THE GROWING CHRISTIAN

JOSEPH T. WATTS, D.D.

NASHVILLE, TENNESSEE
THE SUNDAY SCHOOL BOARD
of the
SOUTHERN BAPTIST CONVENTION

Printed in the United States of America
5.AT54R.R.D.

CONTENTS

ABOUT THE AUTHOR

Joseph T. Watts was born a twin in 1874, at Raleigh, North Carolina, and was brought up a Roman Catholic. He and his brother were coverted in their middle teens.

Dr. Watts worked as a stenographer in various law offices and as a court reporter, until he entered the railroad business, serving as secretary to traffic officials, becoming in 1900 a traveling freight agent.

While a young deacon of a Louisville church he was president of the B.Y.P.U. and later was president of the B.Y.P.U. association of that city, also corresponding secretary of the B.Y.P.U. of the South.

While located in Jackson, Mississippi, in his position with the Illinois Central Railroad, he felt called to the ministry, leading to his ordination at Jackson, and his entrance upon his first pastorate at Aberdeen, Mississippi. After a brief pastorate at Aberdeen he became pastor's assistant at the Broadway Church in Louisville, with the privilege of attending the Seminary.

In 1906 he became the first Sunday school secretary in Kentucky and was also active in the work of the state B.Y.P.U.

In 1909 he was called as secretary of the Sunday school and B.Y.P.U. department of the Virginia State Mission Board, where he worked eighteen and one half years. He was given the D.D. degree by Wake Forest College in 1916.

In 1927 Dr. Watts became general secretary of the Maryland State Mission Board, in charge of mission, Sunday school, and B.Y.P.U. work. He retired in 1948 and subsequently completed his history of Maryland Baptists under the title *The Rise and Progress of Maryland Baptists,* which was published by the State Mission Board, in April, 1953.

FOREWORD

In a time when the churches are confronted, as never before, with the fact that large numbers of their members are not vitally interested in the work of Christ's kingdom, are derelict in the matter of attendance upon public worship, and cannot be depended upon to contribute of their means to the support of the church and the denominational causes for which it has responsibility, it is imperative that active members should address themselves to the ways and means by which large improvement in our fellowship may be realized.

It is believed that the adult division of the Baptist Training Union offers large opportunities for the training of many members, who, by reason of their own neglect or that of others, are found lacking in church interest and efficiency, although many of them have been professed Christians a number of years. As the churches must not allow themselves to become indifferent to those who have never exercised evangelical faith but rather are expected to continue giving to all such the gospel according to its fundamental content urging on their part acceptance of Christ, so also they must not relax their efforts to bring all church members into co-operative relationships in the church, looking toward their growth in Christian character and spiritual service.

With these ends in view THE GROWING CHRISTIAN has been written. The hope is expressed that by a renewal of church effort through the Adult union many inactive, careless, and undeveloped Christians may be brought under teachings and influences which the Master may use to awaken in them a hunger to be more Christlike and to become more useful in the great work which has been committed to his followers.

JOSEPH T. WATTS

CHAPTER I

THE NEW LIFE BEGUN

He was an outstanding physician and surgeon. He attended a church ten years without meeting the pastor and fifteen years without putting his letter in. He sat on the back seat as an observer, never dreaming that he could have a part in the work of God's kingdom. Being invited to the Young People's union, there being no Adult union at the time, he went and caught a vision of service. He at once united with the church he was attending, served as Bible drill leader of the union several years, is now a deacon in the church and is also president of the district association, comprising thirty-two churches, in one of our largest cities.

The purpose of this book is to open a like vision to many other Christians and help them to grow in useful service. Since those for whom this study is primarily intended are church members, it is assumed that they are Christians. But as Christians are exhorted to make their calling and election sure (2 Peter 1: 10), it will be helpful to review the initial experience of grace, with its background of religious nurture.

I. BACKGROUND OF RELIGIOUS NURTURE

The great majority of church members made their profession of faith early in life, principally between the ages of twelve and twenty, although not a few had that experience earlier than twelve, and there are many who could testify to such an experience in adulthood. It must not be overlooked that God is willing to save persons of every age. "The Lord . . . is longsuffering to youward, not wishing that any should perish, but that all should come

to repentance" (2 Peter 3: 9 ASV). It has been well
said, "While the lamp holds out to burn the vilest sinner
may return."

1. *The Home*

Early training has much to do with the practices of
Christians in adult life. Missionaries in foreign lands
tell of the difficulties encountered in dealing effectively
with adult converts, and of the slowness of their progress
in the Christian life. On the other hand, it is much easier
to train the young, who, before they were led to make
a confession of faith, had careful instruction in the Scriptures. It was so with Timothy, Paul's "son in the gospel"
of whom he wrote, "having been reminded of the un-
feigned faith that is in thee; which dwelt first in thy
grandmother Lois, and thy mother Eunice; and, I am
persuaded, in thee also" (2 Tim. 1: 5 ASV). As there is
no effective substitute for the religious home it behooves
every Christian parent to meet his or her responsibility,
both by precept and example, with reference to the children with whom God has blessed the home. Surely, adult
Christians who had such a heritage and environment
should be thankful. Recollections of religious home life
are most precious! And those who were among the underprivileged as to religious nurture should realize the natural handicap under which they are running the Christian
race and give themselves all the more to those exercises
which are necessary to the building of strong Christian
character.

2. *The Sunday School*

Next to a properly conducted Christian home, the
great majority of our readers will testify to the gracious
influence of the Sunday school on their lives. Even the
best Christian parents have long realized the value of
systematic Bible study under Sunday school auspices. It
is estimated that at least 85 per cent of all those who
come into the churches by confession of faith have
been students in the Sunday school. There are some edu-

cational experts who are now finding serious fault with the Sunday school, some going so far as to claim that the institution is "a liability rather than an asset" to the churches. But, while we freely admit the weaknesses of the Sunday school of today, it is still true that most adult Christians hold it in high esteem because of their recollections of consecrated men and women who taught them the Bible and had to do with leading them to Christ. And that which some Sunday school teachers lacked in knowledge and skill was made up in personal piety and love for their pupils. All honor to the army of Sunday school teachers, thousands of whom are highly trained, who have labored to supplement the teaching of the Christian home or to overcome in underprivileged pupils the handicaps with which they came to Sunday school.

The Extension department of the Sunday school has done much to hold to Bible study many who, for various reasons, are unable to attend the Sunday sessions.

3. *Church Attendance*

Those adult Christians who mean most to the churches today are those who were led by parents and Sunday school teachers to love the house of God, attending from early childhood upon public worship. In bygone days parents and children were accustomed to sit together in the family pew. Others had the privilege of sitting with their Sunday school teachers, a practice which might profitably be revived. When protracted meetings were held, the non-church members, young and old, were accustomed to attend upon the preaching of the gospel. All of this made it easier to bring the unsaved to a personal experience of grace. "How then shall they call on him in whom they have not believed? and how shall they believe in him of whom they have not heard? and how shall they hear without a preacher?" (Rom. 10: 14).

A number of years ago Sunday school workers were rudely awakened to find that church attendance upon the part of Sunday school pupils, even those who were professed Christians, had waned. Roger Babson points out that only 30 per cent of the Protestant church members of America attend Sunday worship. If he is correct the number of dependable Christians is tragically small. Much success has attended the introduction of the Six Point Record System, by which, through the emphasis placed upon "Preaching Attendance," many pupils, those who are church members and those who are not, are now regularly present at worship services. While that system was primarily intended to help the young to form desirable habits, it has also been found of great value in stimulating adults to do the same thing, and particularly so in the matter of church attendance.

The present tendency in some sections to neglect evening worship services may be overcome by enlisting large numbers of our older members in the Adult union. Some will recall the time when the evening services were powerful in evangelism. Then the preachers used the morning services for deepening of the spiritual life of Christians, while at the evening services the way of salvation was proclaimed and many persons were won to Christ. Notwithstanding the sharp competition the churches now meet, especially in towns and cities—the radio, Sunday movies, and social gatherings—the evening attendance is being increased through the operation of Adult unions. At the same time, boys, girls, and young people are found in goodly numbers in the evening church services by reason of the example set before them by older people. While it is true that many of our members do not find it practicable to attend all church services, the conduct of bright and worshipful evening services will continue to attract many persons who might otherwise be led to places of worldly amusement. The churches must practice what Thomas Chalmers called "the expulsive power of a new affection" by overcoming evil with good. (See Rom. 12: 21.)

The Eight Point Record System of the Baptist Training Union, designed to help the evening service, has been widely employed with growing success.

II. The Initial Christian Experience

With most persons, regardless of whether they were converted in childhood, youth, or maturity, the initial experience was simple. In essence it was, humanly speaking, merely laying hold of Christ by the exercise of appropriating faith. Spurgeon said: "There are some sciences that may be learned by the head; but the science of Christ crucified can only be learned by the heart." Trust in Christ, while not the ground of salvation to any, is nevertheless its condition for all, coupled with that change of mind, feeling, and purpose called repentance. Hence all new converts begin the Christian life as "babes," needing to be nourished on the milk of the Word (1 Peter 2: 2). The simplicity of conversion has been used by Satan to keep the lost from accepting Christ, while pride has been an even greater stumbling-block. Jesus said: "Except ye turn, and become as little children, ye shall in no wise enter into the kingdom of heaven" (Matt. 18: 3 ASV).

There are among us today some Christian teachers who have deemed it needful to invent new terms by which to describe the new life in Christ. These people are justifying themselves in eschewing the old terms on the ground that they will not be understood in our day. But it is here submitted that it is as easy to teach a generation the terms our fathers employed, which follow the plain teachings of the Bible, as to teach new terms, however attractive they may sound. Indeed, just as each generation of children must be given the rudiments of education, so every generation should be taught the fundamental doctrines of the Christian faith and become familiar with the "language of Zion."

1. Conviction

Reviewing his initial experience, the Christian will immediately recall that there was conviction of sin. In the old Christian Culture Course of the Baptist Young People's Union of America, this experience was defined as "a painful knowledge of sinful self." Conviction was not merely a feeling of guilt; it was the work of the Holy Spirit (John 16: 8). As the late Dr. E. Y. Mullins wrote, "The sin to which conviction refers is summed up as unbelief, lack of faith in Christ. . . . As faith in Christ is the cure for all sin, so the absence of faith, or rejection of Christ, is an act potential of all other forms of sin." The eminent teacher goes on to show that "the doctrine of conviction should not be made into a stereotyped rule—we must recognize degrees of intensity in the conviction of sin. With some no doubt it is a deep tragedy of the soul. With others it is rather a sense of being out of adjustment with God. Temperaments vary; the experience will vary accordingly. We must make due allowances for variety in the manifestation of the Spirit of God." (See *The Christian Religion in Its Doctrinal Expression.*)

In the light of the foregoing let us say that all who have come to Christ for salvation have felt their need of him, for "They that are whole have no need of a physician, but they that are sick" (Matt. 9: 12 ASV).

The conviction that came to the writer's heart, which was the prelude to the experience of conversion, was closely related to the Word of God, and in his case the Word fell upon virgin soil, for he had received no previous instruction in the Bible, though he was well-instructed in the catechism of the church that he attended. This is not to lose sight of other influences of the Holy Spirit which had to do with his being convinced that there was "something wrong with us inside." It is obvious that unless there is conviction for sin in proper degree, one may easily be led superficially to profess the faith and have no vital experience. Usually such persons become merely nominal Christians and in the course of time they cease to attend church services and lapse into utter indifference.

2. *Repentance*

We now consider the experience of turning from sin to God through faith in Christ as the Saviour and Lord. The Roman Catholic doctrine of repentance is very different from that doctrine as held by evangelical Christians.

In the former view there is contrition, confession, and satisfaction; that is, sorrow for sin, confession to a priest and doing penance as an atonement for sin. (*Vincent's Manual.) In the latter view repentance is a change of mind, involving the emotions and the will. Again quoting Dr. Mullins: "Repentance is the translation of two Greek words in the New Testament. One of these expresses the emotional element in repentance. It means regret. But this regret may be of a godly sort leading to genuine repentance or it may be a regret which produces no moral change. The other New Testament word translated repentance means a change of mind or thought. But the change of mind expressed by this word is more than a mere intellectual change of view. It carries with it the idea of will. It is clear, then, that man's spiritual nature as a whole acts when he repents. It is not one faculty or function of the soul but his entire spirit" (2 Cor. 7: 9-10; Luke 18: 23; Matt. 27: 3; Luke 17:3; Acts 2: 38; Rom. 2: 4; Mark 1: 4-14).

"Conversion is a deep work, a heart work. It goes throughout the mind, throughout the members, throughout the entire life" (ALLEINE).

Repentance is a continuing experience. Whenever through the weakness of the flesh there is the commission of sin, there must be a turning from sin; with the Christian not merely because he recognizes that the law of God has been broken, but because sin with him is the violation of his relationship to God as Heavenly Father. The sin of a Christian is worse than that of an unbeliever, for it is a sin against love.

3. Faith

Scriptural repentance always results in turning to Christ. No one truly repents toward God who fails to turn to Christ in faith. This faith is not a mere intellectual acceptance of the gospel, but is an appropriation of Christ's work on the cross, by which one comes to rely upon Christ for salvation. In a little book entitled *Faith

*Out of print.

and the Faith, T. T. Eaton says: "Thirty years ago I advocated making an English verb *faithe* to correspond with the noun *faith*, just as believe corresponds with belief. The lack of such a verb has led to confusion and misunderstanding. Years afterwards in reading Shakespeare's *King Lear* I found Edmund saying to Gloucester, 'Make thy words faithed.' Belief is the assent of the mind—faith is the consent of the heart, including the will. Belief is speculative, faith is operative. Belief accepts, faith acts." And this faith is also continuous, or as we may have sung, "Believe and keep right on believing."

We have thus reviewed the Christian's initial experience on the human side, although, of course, the whole experience is all of grace; for no one ever comes to Christ except as he is divinely drawn. "All things have been delivered unto me of my Father: and no one knoweth the Son, save the Father; neither doth any know the Father, save the Son, and he to whomsoever the Son willeth to reveal him" (Matt. 11: 27 ASV).

4. *The New Birth*

We do well to consider faithfully that miracle of God's grace, or free favor, in what is called regeneration. That word is not often used in the Scriptures for this experience. It is rather a theological term. Only twice does the word "regeneration" occur in the Bible, *first* where it evidently has reference to the consummation of the age (Matt. 19: 28) and *second* where it plainly signifies what evangelical Christians believe concerning the new birth. "Not by works done in righteousness, which we did ourselves, but according to his mercy he saved us, through the washing of regeneration" (Titus 3: 5 ASV). This truth is revealed to us in several ways: A *quickening:* "And you did he make alive, when ye were dead through your trespasses and sins" (Eph. 2: 1 ASV); a *translation:* "Who delivered us out of the power of darkness, and translated us into the kingdom of the Son of his love" (Col. 1: 13 ASV); a *renewal:* "Seeing that ye have put off the old man with his doings, and have put on the new man, that is being renewed unto knowledge after the image of him that created him" (Col. 3:9-10 ASV). These passages clearly show that the experience they describe is that which Jesus taught Nicodemus when he said, "Except one be born anew, he cannot see the kingdom of God" (John 3: 3 ASV).

The necessity for this experience may be stated also in a threefold way:

(1) Because of natural depravity. In Paul's epistle to the Galatians the works of the flesh are stated (Gal. 5: 19-21), so that "he who runs may read." That is a picture of the human heart untouched by divine power.

(2) Because the promises of God are to his spiritual children. "If children, then heirs; heirs of God, and joint-heirs with Christ" (Rom. 8: 17). "He shall receive the crown of life, which the Lord hath promised to them that love him" (James 1: 12).

(3) Because of natural inability to worship God. "God is a Spirit: and they that worship him must worship in spirit and truth" (John 4: 24 ASV). The word "worship" is composed of two words: worth and ship. Those who worship God own his *worthship*. Only those whose minds are illuminated by the Holy Spirit can know his worth, the attributes of his nature.

A prominent member of one of our Louisville churches, now deceased, a German, thus testified in a gathering of Americans in attendance upon the Baptist World Alliance at Stockholm: "I was born first in Germany. I was born second in Louisville, Kentucky. If I had been born only once I should have to die twice, but as I have been born twice I shall have to die only once."

The evidences that one has been born from above are:
a. Faith in Jesus Christ. "Whosoever believeth that Jesus is the Christ is begotten of God" (1 John 5: 1 ASV).

b. Fruit of the Spirit. "The fruit of the Spirit is love, joy, peace, longsuffering, kindness, goodness, faithfulness, meekness, self-control" (Gal. 5:22-23 ASV).

c. Fellowship. "We know that we have passed out of death into life, because we love the brethren" (1 John 3: 14 ASV).

Christians have the "family feeling." It was said of the apostolic Christians, "See how they love one another." And again John says, "Beloved, let us love one another: for love is of God; and every one that loveth is begotten of God" (1 John 4: 7 ASV).

Looking back upon our own conversion we will recall that the love of sin was removed and the love of righteousness was implanted in the soul. A life of holiness as an ideal was begun in us. As Dr. J. M. Pendleton says, "Regeneration is the implantation of the bulb of eternal life." That this experience was necessary to salvation should be clear to everyone, not as in any way connected with baptism, except as that beautiful ordinance pictures to the world what has taken place in the heart. The reader will recall that it was as a Christian that he was received by the church as a candidate for baptism, and that his reception into church membership was conditioned on his baptism. Thus in baptism the Christian was symbolically buried with Christ—and raised to walk in newness of life (Rom. 6: 1-7).

5. Justification and Adoption

Another experience that came at conversion was that of being "justified." As Paul says, "Therefore being justified by faith, we have peace with God through our Lord Jesus Christ" (Rom. 5: 1). Justification is the act of God by which he counts one to be righteous because of his standing in Christ; not that the justified one is righteous in the sense of holiness, but by faith in Christ sin is not reckoned against him. He is no longer under the law. Christ has become the end of the law to everyone that believeth. When Martin Luther, climbing Pilate's staircase in Rome on his knees, suddenly realized that "The just shall live by faith," he did not invent a new teaching, he merely discovered for himself the doctrine that was embedded in the Scriptures of the Old and New Testaments, and proclaimed especially by Paul. Even the Old Testament heroes were justified by faith as shown in Romans 1 to 11 in general and 5 in particular (see also Heb. 12). There is much confusion concerning this doctrine. It is a strong temptation for men to believe that good works have to do with their acceptance with God. Only as we take the Scriptures for our guidance are we able to overcome the temptation to attempt self-justification. No better way has been found to express this glorious truth than the lines:

> Near, so very near to God
> Nearer I cannot be
> For in the Person of His Son
> I am just as near as He.

But as Dr. A. H. Strong well says: "Justification is more than remission or acquittal. The justified person receives not only remission of penalty, but the rewards promised for obedience. This restoration to favor viewed in the aspect of renewal of a broken friendship is denominated reconciliation; viewed in its aspect as a renewal of the soul's true relation to God as a father, it is denominated adoption."

Adoption was an idea derived from Roman law. Paul borrows it to express his idea of the gospel (Rom. 8: 15, 21, 23; Gal. 4: 5-6). By adoption a son was received into the Roman family with all the rights of the true son. So also by adoption we are received into God's family with all the rights of the household. "For ye are all sons of God, through faith, in Christ Jesus" (Gal. 3:26 ASV).

III. CHURCH FELLOWSHIP

1. *Our Covenant*

When we became Christians, were baptized, and given the right hand of fellowship, we voluntarily entered into covenant with the other members of the church. "You will desire to make the most of this new relationship."

It will refresh our minds to read the covenant in general use in the churches:

"Having been led, as we believe, by the Spirit of God to receive the Lord Jesus Christ as our Saviour; and, on the profession of our faith, having been baptized in the name of the Father, and of the Son, and of the Holy Ghost, we do now, in the presence of God, angels, and this assembly, most solemnly and joyfully enter into covenant with one another, as one body in Christ.

"We engage, therefore, by the aid of the Holy Spirit, to walk together in Christian love; to strive for the advancement of this church, in knowledge, holiness, and comfort; to promote its prosperity and spirituality; to sustain its worship, ordinances, discipline, and doctrines; to contribute cheerfully and regularly to the support of the ministry, the expenses of the church, the relief of the poor, and the spread of the gospel through all nations.

"We also engage to maintain family and secret devotion; to religiously educate our children; to seek the salvation of our kindred and acquaintances; to walk circumspectly in the world; to be just in our dealings, faithful in our engagements, and exemplary in our deportment; to avoid all tattling, backbiting, and excessive anger; to abstain from the sale and use of intoxicating drinks as a beverage, and to be zealous in our efforts to advance the kingdom of our Saviour.

"We further engage to watch over one another in brotherly love; to remember each other in prayer; to aid each other in sickness and distress; to cultivate Christian sympathy in feeling and courtesy in speech; to be slow to take offense, but always ready for reconciliation, and mindful of the rules of our Saviour, to secure it without delay.

"We moreover engage, that when we remove from this place, we will as soon as possible unite with some other church, where we can carry out the spirit of this covenant, and the principles of God's Word."

2. *Our Attitude*

The covenant is not a law or set of rules imposed from without, but is the teaching of Scripture put in the form of a covenant for one's edification. A church has the right to exclude from its fellowship those who continue, after due attention, to walk at variance with the covenant under which they were admitted to membership.

Surely growing Christians will be found to be those who have taken the church covenant seriously and are undertaking to order their lives in accordance therewith.

Many churches have the covenant read at business meetings, and on all occasions when the hand of church fellowship is to be extended to new members. It will also be found in many hymnbooks, and in pamphlets and books intended for church members. It should never be allowed to be forgotten. Occasional prayer meeting addresses on the church covenant will give opportunity for expounding its contents. The Adult unions may do much to make this expression of our fellowship obligations of spiritual benefit to many.

3. *Our Relationships*

"If we walk in the light . . . we have fellowship one with another" (1 John 1: 7).

The members of Christ's body are "fellowheirs" (Eph. 3: 6); "fellowcitizens" (Eph. 2: 19); "fellowworkers" (Col. 4: 11); "fellowhelpers" (3 John 8); "fellowservants" (Col. 1: 7; 4: 7; Rev. 6: 11).

SUGGESTIONS FOR FURTHER STUDY AND DISCUSSION

1. What steps should be taken to lead church members to observe the family altar?
2. What can be done in the home to supplement and help the instruction and training of the Sunday school and Training Union?
3. The kind of preaching needed today.

OUTLINE

INTRODUCTION

I. BACKGROUND OF RELIGIOUS NURTURE
   1. The Home
   2. The Sunday School
   3. Church Attendance

II. THE INITIAL CHRISTIAN EXPERIENCE
   1. Conviction
   2. Repentance
   3. Faith
   4. The New Birth
   5. Justification and Adoption

III. CHURCH FELLOWSHIP
   1. Our Covenant
   2. Our Attitude
   3. Our Relationships

CHAPTER II

GROWTH IN GRACE

What a tragedy is the undeveloped Christian! We pity a human being who shows evidence of arrested physical or mental development. How much more serious it is to find a Christian who has failed in the development of Christian character. Peter admonished his readers to "grow in the grace and knowledge of our Lord and Saviour Jesus Christ" (2 Peter 3: 18 ASV).

That churches carry on their rolls many nominal members clearly indicates the great need of efforts toward Christian growth. That this was true in early Christian history is shown by the declaration, "For when by reason of the time ye ought to be teachers, ye have need again that some one teach you the rudiments of the first principles of the oracles of God; and are become such as have need of milk, and not of solid food" (Heb. 5: 12 ASV).

Mr. Spurgeon used to say, "Some Christians are like wasps—they are as big when they are born as they ever are."

With proper emphasis given to winning souls to Christ, ministers, teachers, and personal workers should be diligent in dealing with the new-born in the kingdom, that they may become strong Christian characters. To bring multitudes to baptism and then lose sight of them is a spiritual tragedy. Pastors are undershepherds, called by the Holy Spirit "to feed the church of the Lord which he purchased with his own blood" (Acts 20: 28 ASV). Christ admonishes them, "Tend my sheep" (John 21:16 ASV).

The Adult union was inaugruated for the purpose of aiding Christians in mature life to secure such training as may be needed to enable them to grow in personal righteousness and service.

"Diligent, persistent study should be given to knowing the weaknesses and imperfections of the church, its problems and responsibilities. Each minister should examine the church of which he is pastor to know the measure in which it conforms to New Testament standards" (G. L. GUFFIN).

And what has been said of ministers can be said in due measure of other responsible Christian leaders—as Sunday school teachers, Adult union officers, etc.

Even the so-called Old School Baptists recognize an obligation to "feed the sheep," although they accept no responsibility for inviting sinners to accept salvation through Christ.

I. CHRISTIAN CULTURE

Christian culture comprehends the scriptural doctrine of sanctification. Again quoting from Dr. Pendleton, "Sanctification is the unfolding of the bulb of eternal life into the full blown flower."

1. *Error of "Perfectionists"*

Because the "perfectionists" have erred in claiming sinlessness as a present blessing, many other Christians have gone to the other extreme and seem content to live, so to speak, in the seventh chapter of Romans, forgetting, or failing to realize, that Paul did not divide this epistle into chapters, and that he proceeded from his apparent spiritual dilemma to his victorious experience as recorded in the eighth chapter; indeed, his words, "Who shall deliver me from the body of this death?" are followed by "I thank God through Jesus Christ our Lord" (Rom. 7:24-25).

Dr. A. J. Gordon said, in his *Ministry of the Spirit:* "If the doctrine of sinless perfection is a heresy, the doctrine of contentment with sinful imperfection is a greater heresy. It is not an edifying spectacle to see a

*Now out of print.

Christian worldling throwing stones at a Christian perfectionist." But no well-instructed Christian will claim to be sinless. Dr. Edward Judson used to say, "There are some people who say they are sinlessly perfect. Now, I will not say they are not good people, but I will say they are not the best people." Dr. Mullins points out the need not only of a "second blessing" but many other spiritual experiences. Perfection is, nevertheless, the Christian ideal: "Ye therefore shall be perfect, as your heavenly Father is perfect" (Matt. 5: 48 ASV).

Unlike regeneration the word sanctification is frequently used in the Bible, sometimes meaning separation, sometimes consecration, and sometimes holiness of character.

Jesus prayed, "And for their sakes I sanctify myself that they themselves may be sanctified in truth" and in the same chapter he prayed, "Sanctify them in the truth: thy word is truth" (John 17:17 ASV).

Paul says, "As ye presented your members as servants to uncleanness . . . even so now present your members as servants to righteousness unto sanctification" (Rom. 6: 19 ASV). He also said, "But now being made free from sin and become servants to God, ye have your fruit unto sanctification" (Rom. 6: 22 ASV). To the Thessalonians he wrote, "For this is the will of God, even your sanctification" (1 Thess. 4: 3).

"This is the climax of Christian experience. In sanctification the Christian acts in conjunction with the Spirit in answering the call of Christ to come up to a higher level of life and service in his Kingdom" (TRIBBLE).

Dr. Tribble goes on to say that the clearest expression of the doctrine is found in John 17. "The answer to his prayer for his disciples could only come through their full sanctification."

2. Need for Full Surrender

One may not even measurably experience scriptural sanctification unless he is willing to surrender completely to Christ. It was Dwight L. Moody who said, "It remains yet to be seen what Christ can do with a soul entirely surrendered to his will." One must not only accept Christ as his Saviour from the condemnation of the law, but he must also accept him as Teacher and Lord, to the end that he may know the will of God for his life and be enabled to overcome sin in the soul. Christian culture is therefore a gradual experience—the work of a lifetime. Christian character is only attained through struggle. "Character comes not by the easy way of wishing. It comes only through work, patience, testing" (SELLERS).

3. Transformation of Character

An inspired recipe for becoming Christlike is given by Paul in his Poem of Transformation. "But we all, with unveiled face beholding as in a mirror the glory of the Lord, are transformed into the same image from glory to glory, even as from the Lord the Spirit" (2 Cor. 3: 18 ASV). Vance Havnor has this to say of the text just quoted:

"It is the law of spiritual reflection and how profound are the truths it holds! For ages men have tried to see God, to find and lay hold upon him. But they have sought along the lanes of their own choosing, and they have ended their quest crying like Job: Oh, that I knew where I might find him! Behold, I go forward, but he is not there; and backward, but I cannot preceive him! But God has manifested himself: The Word has become flesh and dwelt among us. He is not merely mirrored in Christ: our Saviour is Emmanuel—'God with us,' in whom dwells all the fulness of the Godhead bodily. Here is the secret of Christlikeness. It is not gained by meticulous copying of his virtues. If he is only an example, he is the most discouraging person who ever lived for we are hopeless before such perfection. The miracle is done as we behold him. That is the believer's one and only business, to keep focused on Christ. Prayer and Bible study, meditation and practical work, consecration and separation, these are but to keep the life turned toward him that he may work his wonders in and through it. The becoming follows the beholding. The likeness follows the looking. Once we were made in his image. Here we are changed into his image."

The reader will do well to refer to the wonderful story of *The Great Stone Face*, by Nathaniel Hawthorne.

Dr. H. Clay Trumbull called the process of transformation "the holy gaze."

II. PRACTICAL MEANS

Now, while we do not believe that salvation is ministered through sacraments, we do believe in the use of all of the means of grace which aid in Christian culture. Note then some of the things which will help us to keep ourselves in such an attitude as will enable the Holy Spirit to work unimpeded in and through us.

1. *The Devotional Reading of the Bible*

The Word of God is the "nourishing food" of the Christian's life. Here we are not thinking particularly of Bible study, though that is highly important. But the growing Christian needs to *read* the Bible as an act of devotion, just to let God speak through its pages to his heart. Manifestly, such a devotional reading of the Bible will lead to those parts of it which are best suited to feeding the spiritual life. The Bible Reader's Course of the Adult union is recommended for this purpose. In the Adult union, as in other departments of the Training Union, the plan is to lead all the members faithfully to follow the daily Bible readings. The quiz leader, in the weekly drill, makes an effort to bring out in the meetings the principal thoughts embedded in the assignments. Neglect of Bible reading will surely be registered in the life. Christians will become anemic and weak if they fail to read the Bible. No amount of reading other good books will suffice to take its place. Said the psalmist, "Thy word have I hid in mine heart, that I might not sin against Thee," of which Matthew Henry says, "This text tells us of 'the best book, the best place, and the best purpose.' " Henrietta Hall Shuck once suggested to her husband a sermon on excuses made by unbelievers, one of which was "I do not know enough." The answer was, "You have the Bible, which God gave to men to guide them into knowledge of himself and man's obligations to his Creator."

2. Private Prayer

Prayer is the Christian's "vital breath," therefore the growing Christian will pray much. He will pray for himself that he enter not into temptation, that his sins may be forgiven, that he may understand the will of God for his own life, and that the wisdom he needs may be given. "If any of you lack wisdom, let him ask of God, that giveth to all liberally, and upbraideth not" (James 1: 5). He will pray for others, remembering that "the supplication of a righteous man availeth much" (James 5: 16). Especially will the growing Christian pray for the success of the gospel in the hearts of men, at home and abroad. He will not fail to pray for his own church, its pastor, officers, and members generally and for the departments of church activity; for soul-winning efforts of the pastor and others; for the missionaries in the state, in the nation, and in what are called foreign mission fields. A prayer list of these is printed with the Baptist Adult union Bible readings. Thus are made more comprehensive the prayers offered by the various members.

We can never know in our own experience the riches of the Lord unto all that call upon him until our souls have formed the habit of looking to him continually. The fearfully common sin, even among professed Christians, of making the glorious God a convenience or necessity in times of need, when ordinarily the mind is carried like a wind-driven wave hither and thither across the sea of life, may account for the number of prayers that are offered in vain. It is the privilege of every child of God to abide in the Saviour; to walk in the

light as he is in the light; to have fellowship with the
Father and with his Son, Jesus Christ; and to maintain
a communion with the Holy Spirit so intimate and so
endearing that prayer will become as natural as breath-
ing, and almost as constant.

"A Christian servant-girl overheard a number of ministers discussing the text 'Pray without ceasing' (1
Thess. 5: 17) and found that at length they appointed
one of their number to prepare an essay upon the subject to be read at their next meeting. She modestly
expressed surprise to a fellow-servant that they should
take so much time about a passage of Scripture so plain
and simple; and her remark having reached the ears of
one of the ministers he asked her why she thought it easy
to understand the text. She replied with humility that
it seemed to her that believers were compelled to pray
without ceasing, for everything they did reminded them
of the Saviour and salvation. 'When, for example,' she
went on to say, 'I open my eyes in the morning. I praise
God who hath shined into my heart to give me the light
of the knowledge of his glory in the face of Jesus Christ.
When I dress, I bless him for having clothed me in the
spotless robe of his dear righteousness. When I wash
my face, I thank him for the precious blood that cleans-
eth from all sin. When I kindle the fire, I think of the
cloven tongues like as of fire, and the Holy Ghost who
came down on the day of Pentecost to dwell with the
disciples of Jesus forever. When I sweep the room, I
ask that the Holy Spirit may remove from me all de-
filement and keep me clean through the Word. When I
eat breakfast, I turn my mind to the Bread of Heaven
that daily nourishes my soul, and thus in all my little
duties there is something that brings Christ before me
and causes me to pray without ceasing.'" (*The Way
Made Plain,* Brookes).

3. *Public Worship*

As already stated in chapter 1, the growing Christian
will make use of opportunities to worship in God's house.

He will not absent himself from these services, without good reason. "I never knew a man or woman who steadily avoided the house of prayer and public worship on the Lord's Day, who did not come to grief and bring other people to grief" (BELLOWS). He will come to church in the spirit of worship, expecting to hear what God has to say through his Word and through the message for his servant who occupies the pulpit. He will worship in song, in prayer, in hearing, and in the contribution of money. Christians should be able to say with the psalmist, "I was glad when they said unto me, Let us go into the house of the Lord" (Psalm 122: 1).

"What greater calamity can fall upon a nation than the loss of worship?" (CARLYLE).

There are those who excuse themselves from public worship by saying that they can worship at home or in God's great out-of-doors. Admitting that God is everywhere and that worship cannot be confined to the house of God, it is still true that neglect of attendance upon public worship usually leads to the neglect of worship anywhere. Worship depends much upon spiritual atmosphere, a condition which can but be found in God's house, a building especially dedicated to worship. Nehemiah sought to maintain public worship, saying, "We will not forsake the house of our God" (Neh. 10: 39). The writer to the Hebrews admonished, "Not forsaking our own assembling together" (Heb. 10: 25 ASV). Pastors know that those who may be depended upon for church support are those who attend the services of the church with reasonable regularity, barring providential hindrances.

4. Religious Conversation

The growing Christian will make much of religious conversation, availing himself of opportunities to hold converse with godly persons. "Then they that feared Jehovah spake one with another; and Jehovah hearkened, and heard, and a book of remembrance was written before him, for them that feared Jehovah, and that thought upon his name" (Mal. 3: 16 ASV). It should be as easy for a Christian to talk about the things of God as to talk about the topics of the day, much of which talk adds nothing to the spiritual life and in many instances actually detracts therefrom. Also he will be helped greatly by having visiting ministers and other Christian workers in his home, that he may profit by their experiences and their knowledge of God. The "prophet's chamber" was doubtless a blessing to those who occupied it, but probably was even more a blessing to the members of the household which maintained such a room. In this day of small homes and apartments, some substitute should be found for that almost extinct institution. Much has been lost to the Christian life by the enforced conformity to present-day modes of living.

"A single conversation across the table with a wise man is worth a month's study of books." (Chinese Proverb.)

5. Reading the Denominational Papers and Other Periodicals

Often it has been demonstrated that the most dependable church members are those who read the denominational papers and other good literature. The denominational papers (there is one in every state in the territory of the Southern Baptist Convention) are indispensable for those who would be informed about the work of the denomination. In these papers the bulk of the space is devoted to news of the kingdom and articles intended for strengthening the spiritual life of the readers. In addition to the information they contain, there is in them much that is highly inspirational and devotional—all of which our people cannot afford to neglect. A canvass of the situation in any field will reveal the fact that those members who are readers of religious papers and magazines are usually those upon whom the church may depend for local and denominational support, both in the matter of active service and contributions of money. In recent years there has been a substantial increase in the circulation of the state Baptist papers. About 931,000 copies go in our homes each week. The slogan of the papers is "A Baptist paper in every home." But many persons who think of the daily newspaper as indispensable utterly ignore religious papers and magazines. Furthermore, it is of vital importance that these papers and magazines be *read* as well as taken.

6. *Bible Study*

The Adult union is provided with appropriate topics for consideration at the weekly meetings, involving the study of the Bible according to the special needs of adults, not as duplicating the systematic study of the Bible in the Sunday school, but as supplementing that plan, and even amplifying such study. The *Baptist Adult Union Quarterly* is rich in the exposition of subjects relating to the Christian life and should be carefully studied by members of the unions, even though one may publicly participate in the discussion of the subject only once a month. The lessons are not treated in the same manner as are the Sunday school lessons, and in no sense do they take the place of such a study. They are suited to the needs of Christians, particularly as those needs relate to individual Christian development, and growth in church and denominational life. There is a distinct advantage for those who avail themselves of the privilege of membership in the union, each member being afforded an opportunity at stated times to contribute to the program and to the development of the lessons, all of which are intended for the deepening of the spiritual life and therefore for growth in grace.

7. *Textbook Studies*

In addition to the weekly subjects as already mentioned, provision is now made for definite studies in Christian culture courses, prepared especially to meet the needs of adults. Those who have had the good fortune to study the textbook courses of the Baptist Young

People's union will find in the Adult courses further incentives toward the study of many vital subjects, such as principles and methods of Adult union work, the Christian home, the New Testament church, the work of the denomination, the Christian and the social order, Christian witnessing, and Christian stewardship and missions at home and abroad, all of which will contribute to their efficiency as church members. Adults should rid themselves of the false notion that only the young may profitably study the textbooks offered by the denomination. When Dr. John H. Vincent was last heard by the writer at Chautauqua Lake, New York, he said to a great congregation, "I am eighty years old but I expect to die learning." Adult Christians may continue to grow until the end of life and be thoroughly furnished unto every good work, if they will persevere in studying the courses offered for their benefit. Never before were there so many opportunities for intellectual and spiritual improvement.

III. CHRISTIAN LIVING

1. *Practicing the Truth*

Christian progress is not made merely by studying subjects, however good, or books, however interesting and useful, nor even by engaging in spiritual discussions, but the lessons learned must be put into practice in everyday life.

Quaint William Secker, an ancient writer and preacher, said, "Super-abundance of privilege demands super-abundance of practice." (*The Nonsuch Professor.*)

"The silent, serene beauty of a holy life is the most powerful thing in the universe next to the might of God" (PASCAL).

2. *Definition of Christianity*

A learned Roman Catholic prelate undertook, over the radio, to define Christianity. He said, "Christianity is a body of doctrines about Christ and a method of liv-

*Out of print.

ing." That definition will surely not be acceptable to Baptists nor to many other evangelical Christians. Christianity is Christ. Our religion is Christo-centric. And the growing Christian, as the late Dr. A. T. Robertson said, is one "who owns Jesus as Lord and Leader and who honestly tries to follow his teaching." Cultural progress then is going forward in Christ. To do otherwise is to stand still and that always means going backward. The growing Christian will be found living the Christ life, best expressed in being engaged in those things which occupied our Lord while he was on the earth. He went about doing good. So must the Christian, not as meriting God's grace, but as the expression of the grace that has been bestowed upon us. When this is done the world will certainly take knowledge of us that we have been with Jesus. Some Christians have found great joy in the employment of Sunday afternoons to visit the sick and lonely, in their own homes or in hospitals. A prominent railroad executive in Virginia made such service the habit of a long life.

3. "Sainthood" Displayed

We must remember that Christ is alive, and as his true followers we are alive in him, as Paul said, "I am crucified with Christ: nevertheless I live." "If ye know these things, blessed are ye if ye do them" (John 13: 17). "A good man does good merely by living" (BULWER).

Sainthood is displayed in practical life. "It is a question of character, not of any form of religious doctrine, freemasonry or worship. Bringing character to a high, full, delicate beauty in daily, practical life is the essential thing" (WATKINSON).

SUGGESTIONS FOR FURTHER STUDY AND DISCUSSION

1. Define the Bible doctrine of sanctification.
2. The place of meditation and reflection in religion.
3. In making decisions for the conduct of their lives, should Christians ask, What would Jesus do?

CHAPTER III

GROWTH IN STEWARDSHIP

The Christian must not only make progress in personal righteousness but also in faithfulness as a steward. While nowhere in the Bible is a steward required to be successful, he is everywhere required to be faithful, and on that basis one is rewarded. The principle of stewardship is deeply embedded in the Scriptures, especially those of the New Testament. In the parable of the unrighteous steward Jesus taught the principle of faithfulness, when in his application of the parable he said, "He that is faithful in a very little is faithful also in much: and he that is unrighteous in a very little is unrighteous also in much. If therefore ye have not been faithful in the unrighteous mammon, who will commit to your trust the true riches? And if ye have not been faithful in that which is another's who will give you that which is your own" (Luke 16:10-12 ASV).

Every church member owes it to himself, to his Lord, and to his church to make a thorough study of the subject of Christian stewardship, for only those who practice that principle can be fully enlisted in the work of the kingdom. The means toward such enlightenment are at the disposal of all our members in the splendid books listed in the several study courses. Adult union members are referred to the excellent books on stewardship in the Adult Union Study Course.

It is unfortunate that the idea has so generally obtained, when stewardship has been mentioned, that it had reference only to the getting and using of money, and the time has come when those who study this subject should discover how broad the term "stewardship" really is and how it ramifies into every phase of a Christian's life.

I. THE STEWARDSHIP OF SELF

Christians, both ministers and laymen, will be unable to meet their responsibilities as church members unless they, like the Macedonians, first give themselves to the Lord. (See 2 Cor. 8:5.)

1. *Full Consecration*

This enforces the need for full consecration to Christ, which is one of the definitions of sanctification as presented in the preceding chapter. Paul, in writing to the Romans, exhorted: "I beseech you therefore, brethren, by the mercies of God, to present your bodies a living sacrifice, holy, acceptable to God, which is your spiritual service" (Rom. 12: 1 ASV).

The bodily powers are always involved in the self idea. We must place "all our being's ransomed powers" at the command of Christ. The feet must be "shod with the preparation of the gospel of peace." The hands must be kept in readiness to serve the Lord whose hands were always busy with deeds of helpfulness. The ears must be kept sensitive to human appeals. The lips must not only "speak no guile," but be ever ready to testify to one's Christian experience. Surely, such a consecration of self will make the Christian willing to go where the Spirit directs and to do what will glorify his name.

2. *Spiritual Separation*

Leaders of Christian work, whether in the pulpit, in the Sunday school, in the Baptist Training Union, or elsewhere, must be ready to pay the price of such service by drawing a clear line of demarcation as between themselves and the world. They should not engage in any activity, whether recreational, business, or political, in which Christ cannot be honored and with which he would not be pleased. They must be in the world but not of the world. The present conformity of Christians

to worldly standards is a great hindrance to the progress
of the kingdom of God. A Christian must decide for
himself what is harmful to his life. Certainly he has no
moral right to abuse his body, which according to Paul
is "a temple of the Holy Spirit." There is a wide difference between pleasure and recreation.

> Live while you live, the epicure would say,
> And seize the pleasures of the passing day!
> Live while you live, the holy teacher cries,
> And give to God each moment as it flies.
> Lord, in my life let both united be;
> I live in pleasure when I live to Thee.
>
> —PHILIP DODDRIDGE

Frequently the practical conclusion that should be
reached by a Christian with reference to questionable
activities must be "better not!"

The scriptural basis upon which a Christian should
decide his course of action on questions where there is
difference of opinion is to be found in Paul's words, "It
is good not to eat flesh, nor to drink wine, nor to do
anything whereby thy brother stumbleth" (Rom. 14:
21 ASV).

3. Faithful Use of Talents

Every Christian is endowed with a talent for some
work and may exert an influence for the good of mankind. There is not an equality of talents. In the
parable of the talents one was given five talents, another
was given two, and another was given one. The principle
of faithfulness is also here taught. The man with five
talents made five talents more. The man with two talents gained other two, but the man with one talent did
that which is still a common fault, namely, he under-
estimated its value and ignored his obligation.

Some Christians have a number of talents. They can
do well a number of things. Others, more limited in
ability, yet render a large amount of service; while many

who can do but little are afflicted with an inferiority complex and do nothing.

Marion Talley possessed a voice which she acknowledged was not her own. She recognized it as entrusted to her by God. She said, "I think of my voice as a gift of God. Of course, it could not have come from any other source, because God is the source of all that is good. I knew a long time ago that it was God's gift. I believe every one of you has a gift of some kind. And I know that if you will use your gift it will grow into a greater one. But you must use it, not waste it. Maybe you will have to make sacrifices for it. I have, but it was worth while. People ask me if I am not afraid when I stand before great audiences. I am not afraid. I was never afraid because it seemed to me that if it was God's gift I had to give them I need not be concerned about their opinion of it. I knew my voice only came *through* me after all. It was from God, and if I just let it come from him through me, to them, it must be perfect, as everything from him is perfect. So I just stood up and sang and people loved it. And the people seemed pleased. I was happy because the great gift that was flowing through me brought with it a joy and exaltation quite apart from the applause and the promises of fame."

Talents must be used or they will not be developed. It behooves every Christian to consider what particular endowment he has and place that at the service of Christ.

There are many of God's children who are not gifted in public work, but if they live righteously they exert a good Christian influence, which is just as powerful as are such activities.

Was it not a great thing for Edward Bok, an immigrant, to give to America such a beautiful gift as the Singing Tower, in Florida? In his book *Two Persons,* he tells how the Dutch Government entrusted to his grandfather the care of a dangerous sand bar off the

*Out of print.

Dutch coast. It was infested with pirates and was as barren of vegetation as the most arid spot on earth. He must establish order and keep the light burning. The government required that of him. But he and his wife were true lovers of beauty and they used the sand bar entrusted to them. They planted it with trees and shrubs and by their persistent work they changed their sand bar into a haven of beauty, where birds rested on their journey across the North Sea, thus saving the lives of thousands. Human beings came also to the sanctuary, from the world over, for inspiration. The message left by these grandparents, "Make the world a bit more beautiful and better because you have lived in it," became Mr. Bok's inspiration throughout his life in America, but he did not find the place to make real their message until he walked one evening from his home at Mountain Lake to Iron Mountain. Standing between those two ancient symbols of man's ideal and his activities, Mr. Bok felt that this mountain was the place to establish a sanctuary for birds and human beings with its beauty, to help each one who saw it to make the world a bit more beautiful and better because he lived in it. His grandparents gave a good account of what was entrusted to them and blessed the world, but more, they influenced Edward Bok to do the same.

II. The Stewardship of the Gospel

The glad tidings are for all mankind, without respect to race, nationality, or environment. Christ is potentially the Saviour of all men. He died for the whole world: "For God so loved the world, that he gave his only begotten Son, that whosoever believeth on him should not perish, but have eternal life" (John 3: 16 ASV).

The apostle Paul referred to himself and his co-laborers as "ministers of Christ, and stewards of the mysteries of God" (1 Cor. 4: 1). And Paul further says, "But we have this treasure in earthen vessels, that the exceeding greatness of the power may be of God, and not from ourselves (2 Cor. 4: 7 ASV).

While there is no doubt that the "mysteries of God" were especially revealed to the apostles, still, as there is no apostolic succession taught in the New Testament such as is held by some ecclesiastics, those mysteries constitute the present stewardship obligation of all true Christians, every one of whom is under obligation to be faithful in the discharge of his duty to pass on the torch to each succeeding generation.

No generation has ever yet been fully evangelized, not even in our own favored country. While Christians are not responsible for saving men, they are bound by their stewardship obligation to do everything in their power so to teach and preach Christ to all men that no one can say in the great day of assize, "No man cared for my soul."

1. *The Content of the Gospel*

The deposit of gospel truth committed to the church is thus stated in the Scriptures:

"That Christ died for our sins according to the scriptures; and that he was buried; and that he hath been raised on the third day according to the scriptures; and that he appeared to Cephas; then to the twelve; then he appeared to above five hundred brethren at once, of whom the greater part remain until now, but some are fallen asleep; then he appeared to James; then to all the apostles; and last of all, as to the child untimely born, he appeared to me also" (1 Cor. 15: 3-8 ASV).

The proclamation of the gospel is a "sweet savor of Christ unto God, in them that are saved, and in them that perish; to the one a savor from death unto death; to the other a savor from life unto life. And who is sufficient for these things?" (2 Cor. 2:15-16 ASV).

2. *Evangelistic Obligations and Opportunities*

As stewardship involves an accounting, Christians should give serious consideration to their evangelistic obligations and opportunities. It is quite insufficient that we hold the body of truth "once delivered to the saints." We must also propagate the truth. When one reflects upon the tragic fact that in the United States not half of our population is Christian under any denominational name, it is not difficult to see that our stewardship of the gospel should thrust us out to make Christ known to the masses of our own people. And when the world is considered, we are at once confronted by the fact that even yet millions of human beings have never heard of Christ. It is even possible for church members to be missionary, in the sense of giving support to missions in foreign lands, and yet be utterly neglectful of the lost in their own homes and communities. In apostolic times the followers of Christ were persecuted and they were "all scattered abroad throughout the regions of Judea and Samaria, . . . Therefore they that were scattered abroad went every where preaching the word" (Acts 8:1, 4). Not in recent times have American Christians been called upon to suffer persecution for their faith, although our brethren in some other lands are passing through terrible experiences. Surely there rests upon Christians who may represent Christ among the lost without hindrance from any source, the necessity to bear witness in season and out of season, to the power of the gospel.

III. THE STEWARDSHIP OF TIME

Every man must give account to God for the use he makes of his time. If Jesus had to say "that every idle word that men shall speak, they shall give account thereof in the day of judgment" (Matt. 12: 36), it follows there must be an accounting for the wasted time involved in the business of living.

1. *Numbering One's Days*

Moses prayed, "So teach us to number our days, that we may get us a heart of wisdom" (Psalm 90: 12 ASV). There the span of life is stated as threescore years and ten, and because of the brevity of earthly life as compared with eternity, it behooves responsible souls to economize time for the glory of God, with whom "A thousand years in thy sight are but as yesterday when it is past, and as a watch in the night" (Psalm 90: 4).

2. *The Sabbath Day*

The Creator of the universe, in whom is infinite wisdom, rested from his work of creation on the seventh day. When the Commandments were given through Moses on Sinai, the principle of one day in seven was announced in the words: "Remember the sabbath day, to keep it holy. Six days shalt thou labor, and do all thy work; but the seventh day is a sabbath unto Jehovah thy God: in it thou shalt not do any work, thou, nor thy son, nor thy daughter, thy man-servant, nor thy maid-servant, nor thy cattle, nor thy stranger that is within thy gates: for in six days Jehovah made heaven and earth, the sea, and all that in them is, and rested the seventh day: wherefore Jehovah blessed the sabbath day, and hallowed it" (Ex. 20: 8-11 ASV).

3. *The Lord's Day*

Christians, divinely guided, adopted the first day of the week as their sabbath, in commemoration of the resurrection of Christ. The Sunday of the calendar is to Christians the Lord's Day. For long years, in Christian lands, the Lord's Day was kept reasonably free from commercialization and worldly occupations. The writer recalls a time when comfort was found in America in the fact that the "Continental Sabbath" was three thousand miles or more from our shores. However, early in the last century violations of the civil sabbath began to be more or less prevalent, resulting in such a movement as "The Lord's Day Alliance" in an effort to protect the Christian citizenship of the country from the growing violation of the Sunday law.

On January 10, 1844, the Hon. Willard Hall, judge of the District Court of the United States for the Delaware district, delivered a notable address in Baltimore, in which he said:

"We cannot escape the conclusion that the observance or neglect of the Sabbath must have an important bearing upon the condition of men; that it is an institution operating with direct effect upon the social and civil status of individuals and communities; that it must have been designed to answer some great purpose; and that by so abusing the Sabbath as to defeat this purpose, we cast away a means, the faithful use of which would be productive of great good."

In the book, *The Day of Worship,* the renowned surgeon, the late Dr. Howard A. Kelly, said, "That nation which has no Lord's Day and that one, which having received it, desecrates it, soon loses all moral stamina, all knowledge of the very meaning of righteousness, and though it continues to exist in name, is spiritually dead."

Public sentiment has gradually crystallized into a very liberal attitude on the subject of Sunday, until now the moving pictures are open on Sunday, baseball and other sports are carried on, many businesses are wide open, and we find ourselves in a most difficult position with reference to its Christian observance. Many city churches are hampered in conducting Sunday evening services, and our people are tempted on every hand to join with the non-Christian world in abusing the day which should be kept holy.

"The Sunday is the core of our civilization, dedicated to thought and reverence—it invites to the noblest solitude and to the noblest society" (EMERSON).

There is no disposition here to advocate church rules with reference to the use of the Lord's Day, but as we are the stewards of that day it can be said without fear of successful contradiction that Christians should apply to their conduct Christ's own words, "It is lawful to do well on the sabbath days." If every Christian, when considering the use of Sunday, will ask himself the question, How may I spend the Lord's Day in such a way as

*Out of print. See your church library.

to be well pleasing unto God? it will not be difficult to reach a solution of the Sunday problem.

Unless Christians may be depended upon to use the Lord's Day for rest, worship, and service to humanity, we have no right to expect a sinful world to protect for us the Christian Sunday. It should be clearly understood that Christians may not properly demand that the state give us a day of worship; we only expect the state to protect the *civil* sabbath, thus giving opportunity to Christian people, and others who are friendly to Christian work, to use the day without the interference of the state and also without the competition which is now found on every hand by those whose principal object seems to be to make money.

"Sunday is the golden clasp that binds together the volume of the week" (LONGFELLOW).

In recent years the blessing of work has come to all the people who were willing to work. Ruskin says: "Indeed the fact is that there are idle poor and idle rich. Many a beggar is as lazy as if he had ten thousand a year, and many a man of larger fortune is busier than his errand boy."

Roger Babson, in his chapter in the book already mentioned, *The Day of Worship,* says, "I have often put the direct question to business leaders, men who are at or near the tops of their respective industries, asking them to tell me their attitude toward Sunday observance. I find that nearly all of these men have come from religious families in which Sunday observance was both principle and practice. Even more significant is the information that the majority of these men have not forsaken the teachings of their youth, but have remained to this day consistent followers of this fundamental. Analysis of their lives shows that they have respect for the day and depend upon it as a source of guidance and inspiration. The big men of business testify that there

*Out of print.

is a remarkable connection between a righteous six days and a religious seventh."

It may be said that as Christians, there is always an abundance of work to be done through the churches for which there is a constant demand for laborers. As Chalmers said: "A Christian's spirituality will depend as much upon his work as his work upon his spirituality." Is it not true that if we shall "seek first his kingdom, and his righteousness; all these things shall be added" (Matt. 6:33)?

"The law of nature is, that a certain quantity of work is necessary to produce a certain quantity of good of any kind whatever" (RUSKIN).

IV. THE STEWARDSHIP OF POSSESSIONS

In his *The Larger Stewardship*, Dr. Charles A. Cook says, "If a man is a faithful steward of his personality, his talents, his calling, he must necessarily be a good steward of his possessions for personality and possessions cannot be divorced. A man cannot be a true steward for God of the one and not of the other." Indeed, what a man earns is really a part of himself. He puts into his earning his mind or his brawn, and the outcome is a part of himself, his very personality. Of course, not all men who work realize this truth. Some are mere "hewers of wood and drawers of water" working for wages only, let us say, rather than working to accomplish a worthwhile task. Such persons are likely to be eye-servants or, at the best, men-pleasers. It matters not what one's occupation may be. Certainly, if he is a Christian he should regard his work, whatever it is, as sacred and unto the Lord.

1. *Recognition of God's Ownership*

The stewardship of possessions includes a recognition of God's absolute ownership, but it goes further. It includes all that is involved in the acquisition of our possessions and in the administration of all that we have acquired. A Christian steward must not only use his money rightfully, but he must gain it rightly. It cannot please God for a man to practice stewardship in the matter of giving who gains his wealth by sweatshop methods, thereby oppressing the poor.

2. *Tithing and Stewardship*

Tithing is only the first step in giving. As someone well says, "Tithing should only be the gateway to the splendid avenue of an enlarged and consecrated Christian giving." But above this gateway is written this question, Are you walking this highway? It is not likely that one will practice the stewardship principle in its largest significance if he is not willing to practice the principle of tithing, which should be the minimum of giving. Most tithers go beyond that standard of giving and some are known to give all that they make beyond their living expenses.

Roger Babson has worked up some figures on tithing. Said he, "If tithing were in operation it would give the churches of this country an income amounting to about four billion dollars a year. The facts are that the church people of the country are giving less than one per cent of their income to church and missionary work. If this were increased to ten per cent, as the Bible asks, the churches would come into their own in a big way that heretofore they have been able only to talk about." This statement was made several years ago. Today, the churches would receive some eight billion dollars if all their members tithed. Actually, they are receiving about a billion dollars a year.

The true stewardship of possessions reaches its highest expression in sacrificial giving. This is well illustrated by the widow's mite, for in that case she gave all her living. We get our inspiration for sacrificial giving only at the cross of Christ. There, Infinite Love made the supreme sacrifice for us. The service that costs has the highest value. Can we render any spiritual service except at real cost? When Jesus healed the woman who touched the hem of his garment he perceived that "power proceeding from him had gone forth" (Mark 5: 30 ASV).

"The church of Jesus Christ is honeycombed with individuals who claim to love God and to have found salvation in Jesus Christ, but their lives are utterly void of any real acknowledgment of this stewardship. About five per cent of the church members give God a tithe of their money and only about fifty per cent contribute regularly for the support of the local church enterprise and far less proportion give money for the missionary enterprise" (AGAR).

It can be shown that twelve men working five days a week on the wages of a skilled mechanic could give reasonable support to a pastor were all of them to tithe their wages. Indeed, the pastor would have much better support than the average servant of Christ is now getting.

In all that has been said we have sought to indicate that Christians have a relationship to Christ which alone makes it possible for them to be faithful stewards. As Paul says, "Ye are not your own; for ye were bought with a price" (1 Cor. 6:19-20 ASV).

3. The Heart of the Stewardship Principle

The heart of the stewardship principle is expressed in the word "others." The author of the following lines expresses the highest ideal of the true Christian steward:

> Lord, help me live from day to day
> In such a self-forgetful way
> That even when I kneel to pray
> My prayer shall be for—Others.
>
> Help me in all the work I do
> To ever be sincere and true,
> And know that all I'd do for you
> Must needs be done for—Others.

Let "Self" be crucified and slain
And buried deep: and all in vain
May efforts be to rise again,
    Unless to live for—*Others.*

And when my work on earth is done,
And my new work in Heaven's begun;
May I forget the crown I've won,
    While thinking still of—*Others.*

Others, Lord, yes, others,
Let this my motto be,
Help me to live for others,
    That I may live like Thee.
                              CHARLES D. MEIGS

(Used by permission of the Meigs Publishing Company, Indianapolis.)

In his little book, *The True Estimate of Life and How to Live,* Dr. G. Campbell Morgan, in discussing "Redeeming the Time," says, "You are rich as the number of hours you have bought up. Every time you buy up an opportunity for him; every time your life tells upon an ungodly man; every time your dealings with God shine out in some of the activities of your life; every time by sacrifice you influence a soul towards God; in that moment, buying up an opportunity, you invest an hour in God, and with those hours God is making you a fortune. What a day it will be when God gives us back these fortunes!"

SUGGESTIONS FOR FURTHER STUDY AND DISCUSSION

1. What is personality?
2. Define the full meaning of "the gospel."
3. What constitutes desecration of the Lord's Day, and what are its effects?
4. How much of the Lord's Day should be given to church work?

OUTLINE

INTRODUCTION

I. THE STEWARDSHIP OF SELF
1. Full Consecration
2. Spiritual Separation
3. Faithful Use of Talents

II. THE STEWARDSHIP OF THE GOSPEL
1. The Content of the Gospel
2. Evangelistic Obligations and Opportunities

III. THE STEWARDSHIP OF TIME
1. Numbering One's Days
2. The Sabbath Day
3. The Lord's Day

IV. THE STEWARDSHIP OF POSSESSIONS
1. Recognition of God's Ownership
2. Tithing and Stewardship
3. The Heart of the Stewardship Principle

CHAPTER IV

GROWTH IN SPIRITUAL SERVICE

A church is a spiritual organization composed of believers in Christ who have been baptized upon a profession of faith in him, and who have voluntarily banded themselves together for the observance of the ordinances which Christ appointed, and for the spread of the gospel throughout the world. The mission of a church is both cultural and evangelistic, to the end that the saved may be built up in the faith and inspired to carry out the work entrusted to the church by Christ, its head. It is essential that the members of a church find proper spiritual employment, for their own good, the good of others, and the glory of Christ.

While good works have nothing to do with the saving of the soul, salvation being all of grace, yet they are enjoined upon Christians as an expression of their faith. "Faith, if it have not works, is dead in itself." "Show me thy faith apart from thy works, and I by my works will show thee my faith" (James 2:17-18 ASV).

It is indeed sad that, with all the emphasis that is put upon the democracy of the church, such a small proportion of its members are really taking part in its activities. It is frequently difficult to find proper persons to fill the offices of the church in its various departments. The reason for this situation is that relatively few persons have received a practical training such as is offered in the Baptist Training Union. The remedy for this weakness is to be found in increasing the membership of this organization, and in seeking to develop the natural gifts of the members through the splendid program of service which it offers. When that is measurably accomplished the churches will have less difficulty in filling places of responsibility with persons who are likely to be both vitally interested and spiritually effective. There is here special application to the Adult union, for many of our "possibilities" are to be found among those Christians who have not enjoyed the benefits of such training as might have been gained in Junior, Intermediate, and Young People's unions. It frequently becomes necessary to draw from the ranks of these maturer men and women the leadership of the church and its several departments of service.

I. THE PRINCIPLES OF SPIRITUAL SERVICE

A consideration by church members of those principles which constitute the foundation of Christian service is here undertaken.

1. *A Growing Love*

The basis of spiritual service is love for God and an outflowing love for our fellow men. As Paul wrote in his poetic classic, "If I speak with the tongues of men and of angels, but have not love, I am become sounding brass, or a clanging cymbal" (1 Cor. 13: 1 ASV). Service undertaken without love will likely soon become irksome and will not be long continued, unless it be for purely selfish purposes. Like God's love, the love of a Christian for other men is benevolent, willing, and concerned for their highest welfare. Thus one may love those who are not themselves lovely, with a purpose to help them. This love need not be what has been called the love of well-pleasing, and certainly not the love of affection, but it is like the love of God of which we sing, "Love divine, all love excelling."

William Penn said, "Love is the hardest lesson in Christianity, but for that reason it should be most our care to learn it."

2. *A Growing Self-Realization*

No Christian should overestimate himself or his natural abilities, yet no Christian should *underestimate* himself. As Paul says, "I say, through the grace that was given me, to every man that is among you, not to think of himself more highly than he ought to think; but so to think as to think soberly, according as God hath dealt to each man a measure of faith" (Rom. 12: 3 ASV). A growing Christian should be able to say with him, "I can do all things in him that strengtheneth me" (Phil. 4: 13 ASV) which is interpreted to mean that he could do all the things which Christ required of him, for God never requires anything of his children which he is not ready to enable them to perform. God is all-powerful. Of course, he might himself do the things he asks us to do, or he might delegate angels to do them, "but God chose the foolish things of the world, that he might put to shame them that are wise; and God chose the weak things of the world, that he might put to shame the things that are strong" (1 Cor. 1: 27 ASV).

"Activity is God's medicine; the highest genius is willingness and ability to do hard work. Any other conception of genius makes it a doubtful if not a dangerous possession" (McArthur).

As in the field of education, it has been found necessary to provide vocational training for those who are not endowed for purely intellectual pursuits, so the church should undertake to discover the natural bent of its members and give them the needed training along such lines.

3. A Growing Constancy

The growing Christian will not render a vacillating service. As Paul wrote, "And let us not be weary in well doing: for in due season we shall reap, if we faint not" (Gal. 6: 9). Many Christians resolve to be faithful in the discharge of their duties, either in the matter of attendance, service, or giving, but they fail to keep their resolution because, with them, the grace of constancy is lacking. To the Galatians Paul wrote, "Ye were running well; who hindered you?" (Gal. 5: 7 ASV). Church members are greatly needed who can be depended upon in foul as well as in fair weather; who will not forsake the assembly of the saints, who will faithfully stand by the pastor in his arduous work; who will give regularly to the expenses of the church and to missions, and who, when compelled to be absent from the church, will not forget that the work must go on; who will continue steadfastly in prayer; in short, who will at all times be as much concerned about the work of the church as are the pastor and deacons.

The writer vividly recalls that in his boyhood he was thrilled by an old gray horse, whose only work was to operate with his feet the treadmill in which was cut up the feedstuff used in a great livery stable. He did not need to be driven to his post of duty, but at regular times, which he well knew by experience, he would walk out of his stall and into the work expected of him. When witnessing all this there was a boyish response in the nature of a challenge to do at least as well as an old gray horse, for although he was not then a Christian he had learned that he was created in God's image.

4. *A Growing Enthusiasm*

Emerson said, "Nothing great was ever achieved without enthusiasm." Paul exhorts that we should be "fervent in spirit" (Rom. 12: 11). The word "fervent" has in it the idea of enthusiasm to the boiling point. A splendid layman of Louisville, Kentucky, who, though lacking formal education, was a most diligent and effective Christian worker and a most successful soul-winner, once read the twelfth chapter of Romans in connection with a meeting of the Baptist Young People's Association. When he reached the eleventh verse he read it "not slothful in business, *fevered* in spirit, serving the Lord." He had not missed the true meaning of the word. Perhaps one may be enthusiastic only for that which is possible, for that which is reasonable, and for that which is difficult. Certainly that which is too easily achieved offers no particular challenge.

It took enthusiasm to build the Panama Canal. Originally begun in 1881 by a French company under M. de Lesseps, the work went on until 1887, when, after an expenditure of $226,000,000, comparatively little had been accomplished, and operations ceased in 1889. The work abandoned by the French company was taken up by another company but no marked progress was made. The United States Government then had under consideration the building of a canal across Nicaragua, but at this time the French company sold its interest in the Panama Canal to our country for $40,000,000. After some difficulties with the government of Colombia, Panama, in 1903, became a republic, and permission was given to complete the canal. The region was subject to yellow fever, malaria, and other tropical diseases, by which the French working forces had been terribly decimated. In 1904, General William C. Gorgas was sent to the Canal Zone by President Theodore Roosevelt as chief sanitary officer, and victory was achieved in the war for sanitary conditions so that the Canal Zone was made as healthful as any part of the United States. General George Washington Goethals was sent to the Canal Zone in 1907 and made such rapid progress with his task that the Canal was opened for the passage of ships in August, 1914.

The Christian life is not easy, but who could wish to remove all the difficulties? Should we not rather say:

> Sure I must fight, if I would reign;
> Increase my courage, Lord;
> I'll bear the toil, endure the pain,
> Supported by Thy Word.
>
> —Isaac Watts

II. The Privileges of Spiritual Service

1. *Friends of Christ*

By spiritual service we may prove our friendship for Christ. He said, "Ye are my friends, if you do whatsoever I command you" (John 15: 14). General Robert E. Lee is reported to have said in a letter (now proved to be a forgery) that "duty is the sublimest word in the English language." He demonstrated its power in the whole of his military and civil life, but for the growing Christian let it be said that "privilege" is a greater word than duty. Duty is what we owe toward God, toward country, or toward our fellow men, whereas Christian privilege grows out of a spiritual relationship sustained to Christ that cannot be exercised by those who are not Christians.

2. *Representatives of Christ*

By spiritual service we show ourselves to be loyal ambassadors of Christ. We represent him, not as a nation's representative at a foreign court, but at the door of the human heart. No governmental representative occupies a position of such great dignity and honor as does the ambassador of Christ. "We are ambassadors for Christ" (2 Cor. 5: 20). Such a position of privilege and responsibility must be faithfully administered or the Christian will fail to give a proper account of himself.

3. *Channels of Blessing*

By spiritual service we become channels of blessing to others. When Jehovah called Abram from Ur he said: "I will bless thee, and make thy name great; and thou shalt be a blessing" (Gen. 12: 2). The King James Version makes the second part of that passage read "and thou shalt be a blessing," which rendering accords with the latter part of the third verse "and in thee shall all families of the earth be blessed" (Gen. 12:3). The question is properly raised, "Is your life a channel of blessing?"

"Our gifts and attainments are not only to be light and warmth in our own dwellings but are also to shine through the windows into the dark night, to guide and cheer bewildered travelers on the road" (H. W. BEECHER).

Every growing Christian may be a channel of blessing provided he yields himself to God to do the simple services which are possible to all.

(1) *Prayer.*—The growing Christian may be a blessing in prayer, not alone for oneself, but also prayer for others. Such unselfish service reacts for good upon one

who prays. When Job prayed for his friends Jehovah turned his troubles into blessings, for we read that "the Lord gave Job twice as much as he had before" (Job 42: 10). As Austin Phelps says, "Prayer is a power, has a power, not subjective merely. So any unperverted mind will conceive of the scriptural idea of prayer as that of one of the most downright, sturdy realities of the universe. Right in the heart of God's plan of government it is lodged as a power."

The biography of D. L. Moody relates how a shut-in woman in England, having heard of the evangelist's success in America, prayed to God that he might be sent to her people. After a long time Mr. Moody came to her community and a great revival ensued. Its power was traced to the sick woman who had earnestly prayed for his coming.

(2) *Song.*—A Christian may be a blessing in song. If one has a voice and will consecrate it to God, he can use it for God's glory. What would our churches do without gospel music? What could Mr. Moody have done without Mr. Sankey? What could Dr. Torrey have done without Mr. Alexander? Even heathen religious leaders are copying as best they can the singing of Christian people by setting the words of their songs to Christian tunes. Many could testify that their hearts were first opened to the gospel by the singing of some consecrated voice.

Charles E. Cowman spent many years in Japan as a missionary. In his biography he is quoted as follows concerning his wife's conversion in Chicago: "A converted opera singer was to speak and sing. My wife, being interested in music, accepted the invitation and heard the noted leader sing:

> There were ninety and nine that safely lay,
> In the shelter of the fold,
> But one was out on the hills away,
> Far-off from the gates of gold.
>   —Elizabeth C. Clephane

It was like the singing of Paul and Silas in the jail at midnight and was accompanied by a spiritual earthquake which led her heart from its worldly satisfaction. She began dealing with me but I told her that living a Christian life in a train dispatcher's office was an utter impossibility; however, her prayers and continued exhortations were rewarded by my conversion one month later."

(3) *Personal witnessing to the lost.*—A Christian may be a blessing in personal evangelism. We sometimes imagine that the present ineffectiveness of much of the so-called mass evangelism is peculiar to our times. While there were great evangelistic meetings held during the eighteenth and nineteenth centuries, under such men as John Wesley, Charles G. Finney and D. L. Moody, and in the present century great meetings have been held by such men as Geo. W. Truett, R. A. Torrey and J. Wilbur Chapman, it has ever been true that much personal work was necessary to the bringing of souls to Christ. Even on the day of Pentecost under the preaching of Peter, when three thousand souls were added to the church in one day, there is reason to believe that the other apostles and disciples had part in that great ingathering. Certainly in our day, when relatively few unconverted men and women attend evangelistic services, it is needful for every Christian to be ready at all times to bear witness to the power of Christ and to seek to contact the lost and help them to find salvation in Christ. If every member of the Adult unions would earnestly seek to become a winner of souls, our churches doubtless would experience a perpetual revival. The question may properly be raised, whether, without such personal evangelism upon the part of the members of the Adult union and other groups, we are justifying the work of teaching and training. A sincere invitation to the unsaved to come to church services, or to attend a Bible class, may prove a blessing to some life.

A protracted meeting was being held in the Walnut Street Church in Louisville. A timid but consecrated woman responded to the evangelist's appeal to go afield and invite the unsaved to the services. A young man, invited by her, came and was converted. He was none other than George C. Lorimer, who became one of the outstanding preachers of the Baptist denomination, and at a later date was pastor of the Walnut Street Church, Louisville, and of Tremont Temple in Boston.

(4) *Public speech.*—A Christian may be a blessing in public speech. Admitting that not every one has a talent for public speaking and that many must be contented with other phases of Christian service, there are doubtless many men and women who are not using the talent for speaking that God has given to them. This is true especially of many adults who did not receive training for public utterance in the Junior, Intermediate, and Young People's unions. But there are many adults who are greatly needed for public service who can yet equip themselves for the exercise of public prayer, testimony, and address.

There is a great need for those who can occupy worthily the platforms of associations, and of state and Southwide conventions, to participate in the presentation and consideration of denominational work. Of late years, the number of laymen who are thus qualified and who attend such meetings has been entirely too small. The people who attend our denominational meetings are always glad to hear able ministers on the various subjects presented, but this does not alter the fact that there is great need, for many reasons, for consecrated laymen (persons upon whom our missionary and benevolent agencies and institutions must depend largely for financial and moral support) to be heard. A quarter of a century ago it was the custom to place great laymen at the head of our associations and conventions. One recalls how several presidents of the Southern Baptist Convention were laymen, some of them former governors of their respective commonwealths. The question arises whether such material for our highest office is lacking in our day. Certainly it is incumbent upon the churches to develop, through the Adult union and other forms of church life, men who shall be both willing and able to assume places of leadership in the local churches and in the work of the denomination.

It should be understood that after all it is only the overflow of the spiritual life that we really give out to others. At the Feast of Tabernacles, on the last day of the feast, Jesus cried, "If any man thirst, let him come unto me and drink. He that believeth on me, as the scripture hath said, from within him shall flow rivers of living water" (John 7:37-38 ASV). John added a word which all growing Christians should ponder well, when he said, "But this spake he of the Spirit, which they that believed on him were to receive: for the Spirit was not yet given; because Jesus was not yet glorified" (John 7: 39 ASV).

(5) *Administrative work.*—A Christian may be a channel of blessing in administrative work. Many of our members may be fitted for executive duties in the church. Such workers are greatly needed to enable the churches to function efficiently. There are great opportunities in the churches for utilizing such abilities in connection with the duties of deacons, trustees, clerks, treasurers, officers in the Sunday schools, Baptist Training Unions, and for Woman's Missionary Unions and in committee assignments.

There is no reason why a church, because of a vacancy in the pulpit, or the temporary absence of the pastor, should not have public worship if the members of the Adult union are willing to give themselves to the needed training for taking care of such services. There are now many laymen who are able to render this kind of service, but the number can and should be greatly increased through the Adult union.

III. PRACTICAL SUGGESTIONS

1. *Finding One's Place*

No amount of theorizing on the matter of spiritual activities can take the place of practical efforts to help the individual to find a place of service. Those who are responsible for the work of the church in its varied departments and agencies should give earnest prayer and thought to the latent talents of different members and be in position to give definite advice and encouragement.

A pastor in one of our cities could preach well on the subject of service, but when asked by a member, "What may I do?" could only answer, "You must find that out for yourself." There is a very true sense in which that pastor was right, but it is the responsibility of pastors and other leaders to point out avenues of practical service for all those who are willing to work.

2. *Dividing Responsibility*

One of the drawbacks in our churches is the fact that a few willing and more or less capable persons are elected or appointed to practically all the places of usefulness, and that many others, with natural gifts and great possibilities for development, are forced to occupy "back seats," with nothing definite to do. The motto for the church should be "To every man his work." We should carefully avoid allowing cliques to develop in a church, for what will become of the work when the present leaders pass away if we have failed to train others to take their places?

Greater credit belongs to church leaders who succeed in putting many people to work than to those who themselves undertake to do everything that is to be done.

Wise parents direct their children in doing things which they can do, though crudely at the first, looking toward the time when they may do them well. Likewise in the church family various members may and should be put to work in one way or another, letting them learn to do by doing, for self-help is the best help.

3. Developing Adult Leaders

In the Adult union there will be found many men and women who have not been used in the work of the church, but who may be gradually developed to take part not only in the discussions of topics, but also in personal service. They need to be trusted to do things for Christ and the church, and they must be carefully guided in Christian work by those who have had experience. Thus a larger proportion of our membership will be enlisted in various forms of spiritual service, for their own good and the strengthening of the whole organization.

The strong tendency of adult Christians to become absorbed in business, professional, political, and social activities, forgetting their obligation as church members, and in many cases becoming indifferent, joyless, and useless, can be overcome by setting ourselves to the difficult task of training such persons to take part in the work of the church.

Excuses in abundance may be found for not doing church work, but there are many, many examples to show that busy professional and businessmen have found time for Christian service. In truth, the faithful service of many laymen, often at the loss of material gain, is such as should inspire ministers of the gospel, who are supported in their work, to put forth greater efforts to bring in the kingdom.

The question of the Master, "Why stand ye here all the day idle?" should not admit of the scriptural answer, "No man hath hired us."

SUGGESTIONS FOR FURTHER STUDY AND DISCUSSION

1. Contrast "worthy" and "unworthy" motives for church work.
2. What are the essential qualifications for leadership in Christian work?

OUTLINE

INTRODUCTION

I. THE PRINCIPLES OF SPIRITUAL SERVICE

1. A Growing Love
2. A Growing Self-Realization
3. A Growing Constancy
4. A Growing Enthusiasm

II. THE PRIVILEGES OF SPIRITUAL SERVICE

1. Friends of Christ
2. Representatives of Christ
3. Channels of Blessing

III. PRACTICAL SUGGESTIONS

1. Finding One's Place
2. Dividing Responsibility
3. Developing Adult Leaders

CHAPTER V

DISCIPLINARY AIDS TO CHRISTIAN GROWTH

The New Testament church, like the family, has responsibility for the training or discipline of its members. This is true of all the members, the young and the old, but the subject is here presented with reference to those members who are eligible to membership in the Adult union, a department of the Baptist Training Union. The Baptist Adult union has in it great potentialities for the strengthening of the adult part of the church. Admittedly this is a more difficult work than that of the Young People's, Intermediate, or Junior unions. The saying, "You can't teach an old dog new tricks" has in it an element of truth, only it must be borne in mind that adult Christians are not "dogs" but men and women created in the image and likeness of God, and by the grace of regeneration *re-created* unto good works. Whatever one's age may be, even though converted in mature life, he is but a babe in Christ. All Christians may grow and all need spiritual discipline.

But adult Christians must *yield* themselves to necessary discipline if they are to overcome their habits of thought, speech, and action, formed in many instances before they gave themselves to Christ, or contracted in mature life by reason of their own failure or the failure of others to exercise spiritual discipline.

"A man in old age is like a sword in a shop window. Men that look upon the perfect blade do not imagine the process by which it was completed. Man is a sword. Daily life is the workshop and God is the artificer; and those cares which beat upon the anvil, and file the edge, and eat in, acid like, the inscription on the hilt—those are the very things that fashion the man" (H. W. BEECHER.)

I. CONSTRUCTIVE DISCIPLINE

1. *Care in Receiving Members*

If numerous exclusions or "erasures" are to be avoided in the future, more attention must be given to those methods by which new members are received into the churches. Some of the churches are very careful about this matter, requiring applicants for membership to appear before the pastor and deacons or a special committee for the purpose of determining whether their experience and attitude will justify their acceptance by the church; while with some other churches it would appear that many applicants for membership are not dealt with at the outset in such a way as to make them feel the seriousness of the church relationship. If prospective members can be properly impressed with the duties and privileges of church membership, great benefits will accrue both to the new members and to the churches.

A brochure by Dr. J. O. Williams, of the Sunday School Board, entitled "Definite Decisions for New Church Members" will prove most helpful in the matter of giving direction to new members.

2. *Participation at the Lord's Supper*

Churches need to pay closer attention to the observance of the Lord's Supper. Some churches neglect the ordinance and many church members frequently absent themselves from the Lord's table when it is being observed.

While Baptists do not think of the Lord's Supper as a sacrament, conveying grace, still, for a Christian to be obedient to Christ's commands he will gladly participate in that memorial of Christ's death. Those who wilfully stay away from the Lord's Supper will likely be those who are living lives inconsistent with church membership. Jesus said, "This do in remembrance of me." Mr. Spurgeon said, "Those who have forgotten Christ have the greater need to remember him."

3. *Immediate Enlistment*

Our churches maintain Sunday schools, Training Unions, Woman's Missionary Unions, and midweek prayer meetings for the deepening of the spiritual life of their members and for enlisting them in the work of Christ's kingdom. But are not many churches failing to put forth the proper efforts to bring into these organizations and services a larger number of their people, especially those who are most in need of training!

Said Dr. Theodore L. Cuyler: "A very large proportion of the members of our churches count for very little except upon the muster-roll. When that roll is called for practical service they do not answer 'here.' The lamentable statistics of contributions show how small are the pecuniary gifts of these comatose Christians. The true time to enlist a Christian in active service is when he enlists in the visible army of Christ by public profession of faith. If a new convert does not open his lips in some devotional meeting during the first thirty days, he is apt to remain tongue-tied for life. If he or she is not called into some sort of service, then doth he or she become a drone in the hive."

The Adult unions should be active in enlisting tens of thousands of church members in the training they afford. While Southern Baptists have a Sunday school membership of 5,759,128 (1953), they only have 1,849,544 (1953) members of the Baptist Training Unions. The spiritual welfare of many adults demands large numbers of new members in the Adult unions.

II. SELF-DISCIPLINE

1. *Personal Efforts*

Because "self-help is the best help," we turn to the New Testament to discover the manner in which Christian men and women are to co-operate with the Spirit of God in securing spiritual self-discipline.

"What we do upon some great occasion will probably depend on what we already are; and what we are will

be the result of previous years of self-discipline" (LID-
DON).

Paul says, "Know ye not that they that run in a race
run all, but one receiveth the prize? Even so run; that
ye may attain. And every man that striveth in the
games exerciseth self-control in all things. Now they do
it to receive a corruptible crown; but we an incorrup-
tible. I therefore so run, as not uncertainly; so fight
[box] I, as not beating the air: but I buffet [bruise] my
body, and bring it into bondage: lest by any means, after
that I have preached to others, I myself should be re-
jected" (1 Cor. 9: 24-27 ASV).

He exhorted Timothy: "I put thee in remembrance
that thou stir up the gift of God, which is in thee through
the laying on of my hands. For God gave us not a
spirit of fearfulness; but of power and love and discipline" (2 Tim. 1: 6-7 ASV).

A great Christian layman, who gave forty years to the
missionary work of his state, had a way of saying, "I
am very strict with myself but liberal with the faults of
others." The truth is that unless a Christian is willing
to engage in self-discipline, no spiritual discipline on the
part of the church will be effective, with him.

This is by no means to advocate anything akin to the
Romish practice of self-scourging as a means of grace.
Christians are not made strong by betaking themselves
to cloisters and monasteries, and separating themselves
from worldly society that they may become holy; rather
they are to be in the world but not of the world and yet
they are to keep themselves "unspotted from the world"
(James 1: 27).

2. *Overcoming Temptation*

A Christian becomes strong through overcoming
temptations to worldly conformity. He should rely on
the promise of the Bible: "There hath no temptation
taken you but such as man can bear: but God is faithful,
who will not suffer you to be tempted above that ye are
able; but will with the temptation make also the way of

escape, that ye may be able to endure it" (1 Cor. 10: 13).

3. *Courage and Faith*

The story of the three Hebrew worthies, Shadrach, Meshach, and Abednego, as found in the third chapter of Daniel, should strengthen Christian faith. Their behavior "under fire" was not merely an expression of courage; a bad man may have that, but was an expression of great faith. "This is the victory that hath overcome the world, even our faith" (1 John 5: 4 ASV).

Jesus condemned hypocritical fasting when he said, "Moreover when ye fast, be not, as the hypocrites, of a sad countenance: for they disfigure their faces, that they may be seen of men to fast. Verily I say unto you, they have received their reward." But he commended fasting when he said, "But thou, when thou fastest, anoint thy head, and wash thy face; that thou be not seen of men to fast, but of thy Father who is in secret: and thy Father, who seeth in secret, shall recompense thee" (Matt. 6: 16-18 ASV).

4. *Pressing Toward the Goal*

And Paul, who had suffered the loss of all things that he might gain Christ, after he had been a Christian twenty-five years, said, "I press on, if so be that I may lay hold on that for which also I was laid hold on by Christ Jesus. . . . Forgetting the things which are behind, and stretching forward to the things which are before, I press on toward the goal unto the prize of the high calling of God in Christ Jesus" (Phil. 3: 12-14).

"Be always displeased at what thou art, if thou desire to attain to what thou art not; for where thou hast pleased thyself there thou abidest" (QUARLES).

5. *Simple Living*

If the facts were known, there are many Christian men and women in America who live the simple life in order that the causes dear to their hearts may be amply supported.

A Baptist in a Southern city lived in practical poverty, in order that he might leave his little property, valued at $2,500, to his state mission board. His will required the board to keep the fund invested until it reached a value of $10,000 when the income could be used for state mission work. Some years ago that time was reached. What a memorial to a poor man!

6. *Willingness to Be Different*

Self-discipline has a negative as well as a positive expression. Surely the line of demarcation (almost obliterated) between the church and the world, will not be restored except as consecrated Christians are willing to be *different*—a peculiar people—"zealous of good works" (Titus 2: 14).

Paul says: "And be not fashioned according to this world: but be ye transformed by the renewing of your mind, that ye may prove what is the good and acceptable and perfect will of God" (Rom. 12: 2 ASV). On the principle there enunciated Christians will not find it difficult voluntarily to refrain from "fleshly lusts, which war against the soul" from which Peter admonishes them as "sojourners and pilgrims" to abstain (1 Peter 2: 11 ASV). It should not be necessary for a preacher, or Sunday school teacher, or Adult union president to formulate rules for the conduct of Christians. The New Testament is our guide, and it is a book of principles, not rules. But when the church, through its ministers and other spiritually minded members, so interprets those principles as clearly to point the way to Christian living, many persons will be brought to a more consecrated life. All innocent pleasures belong to the Christian for, said Paul, "All things are yours" (1 Cor. 3: 21).

7. *One's Interests the Test*

The test of Christian growth is found in one's daily interests. Christians grow by what they feed upon. Surely, if one's interests during the week days are all in worldly affairs, what he does on Sunday will be permeated by the same thoughts. It is scarcely possible for a Christian to be spiritually alive on Sunday if he is dead to those interests all the rest of the week. One's reading is also a matter for deep reflection. No man will relish the Bible and Bible teaching on Sunday if he has neglected it all the week before and saturated his mind with the questionable, if not actually salacious, books and magazines which fill our book stalls. It is a far cry from the old Sunday school library to the books now popularly read, even by many church members. The growing Christian will discriminate in his reading matter as well as in other forms of recreation and amusement.

And as Paul wrote, "Whatsoever things are true, whatsoever things are honorable, whatsoever things are just, whatsoever things are pure, whatsoever things are lovely, whatsoever things are of good report; if there be any virtue, and if there be any praise, think on these things" (Phil. 4: 8).

III. CORRECTIVE DISCIPLINE

As no home, having children under its care, can be properly conducted without corrective discipline, so it is needful for such discipline to be exercised by the church, the family of believers in Christ.

1. A Grave Problem

Just how to do the work of corrective discipline is a grave question.

It was done so unwisely in some periods of our history as a denomination that many churches have practically ceased to practice any real discipline. Corrective discipline is not to be done in a harsh manner and it will only succeed when done in connection with constructive discipline, and with those who are true Christians, gladly willing to practice self-discipline.

However, if the leadership of a church will keep itself in sympathy with the social and spiritual needs of the membership, a way will be found to apply such correctives as may be needed.

The author well recalls that when he had been a Christian and a church member only a few years, he yielded to the temptation to "sign up" for dancing lessons under an itinerant Italian dancing master. "Pumps" were purchased and everything was in readiness for him to take his first lesson, when he was asked by the Sunday school superintendent to come to his office. The superintendent was also a deacon and his wife was the youth's teacher. The interview was very brief. The good deacon said, "Joe, I understand you are going to take dancing lessons!" The youth answered, "Well, I was, but I'm not," and that was the end of dancing lessons for that boy.

2. *Overcoming Evil with Good*

There is a responsibility resting upon the churches to "overcome evil with good" (Rom. 12: 21) by providing an adequate social program, and such a program is needed for adults as well as for young people. It will be apparent to any practical observer of human conduct that much of the worldliness of the young is due to the bad examples set before them by adults.

Paul wrote to Titus: "But speak thou the things which befit the sound doctrine [teaching]: that aged men be temperate, grave, sober-minded, . . . in all things showing thyself an example of good works" (Titus 2: 1-2, 7 ASV).

Corrective discipline is also needed in connection with many church members who do not contribute to church and denominational support. Giving as an act of worship is the acid test of the Christian life for those who have anything to contribute. Nongiving members are almost universally nonattending members.

3. *Noncontributing Members*

A church is derelict in its duty toward its members when it permits them to go on year after year as noncontributors, without any real effort being made to show them the better way. It requires courage to say to such members what is needful, and not every active member has the tact to do it, but it should be undertaken for the good of the unenlisted member. A city church observed homecoming day with attractive exercises, including a roll call. Not one-half the members answered to their names. It was brought out there that only one-fourth of the membership were contributors of record to the missionary program of the denomination. No wonder it was difficult for that church to reach its modest objective for missions. The church covenant quoted in chapter 1 definitely commits each member to contribute to church support.

IV. PUNITIVE DISCIPLINE

Dr. E. C. Dargan, in his *Ecclesiology*, says, "It is a mournful fact that in many of our churches today apostolic discipline may be said not to exist, and some few apologists for this state of things might doubtless appear; but surely most of our churches would consent in theory if not in actual practice to a pure and correct discipline."

1. *Exclusion for Cause*

It sometimes becomes necessary to exclude a member for an offense against society, or for conduct unbecoming a Christian. Paul commanded the church at Corinth to withdraw fellowship from a member who was found guilty of incest. Apparently the church lacked the moral courage to take proper action until Paul intervened with his apostolic authority. That it was the right thing to do is shown by the sequel, where Paul also intervened to induce the church to forgive the offending brother and restore him to fellowship. Knowing that he had been excluded and because he was really a saved man he came back like a sheep bleating at the door of the sheepfold.

In 2 Thessalonians the apostle commanded the church in the name of the Lord Jesus Christ, to withdraw from every brother who walked disorderly. Said he, "And if any man obeyeth not our word by this epistle, note that

*Now out of print.

man, that ye have no company with him, to the end that he may be ashamed. And yet count him not as an enemy, but admonish him as a brother" (2 Thess. 3: 14-15 ASV).

2. *Converting the Sinner*

In James we read, "My brethren, if any among you err from the truth, and one convert him; let him know, that he who converteth a sinner from the error of his way shall save a soul from death, and shall cover a multitude of sins" (James 5: 19 ASV).

3. *A Great Fault*

In former years the churches were careful to exercise punitive discipline toward members who were guilty of theft, drunkenness, profanity, and immorality, but because little discipline of any kind is now undertaken many churches are led to overlook even the grosser sins.

Great wisdom, patience, and tact are necessary if the purity of the churches is to be preserved, without doing harm to those not themselves the subjects of discipline, who will be affected by drastic actions toward others. Still it remains true that the churches are under obligation to deal faithfully with all of their members and should face their duty with courage.

V. DISCIPLINE BY ERASURE

1. *Effort to Arouse Interest*

In the judgment of the writer the name of no member should be erased from the roll until every reasonable effort has been made to arouse in him a vital church interest. This will involve careful visitation by the pastor and other influential members with a view of doing such persons spiritual good. Further, when names are removed from the roll, the persons affected should be frankly and tenderly informed of it, in the hope that their hearts may be moved to a desire for renewal of church fellowship.

2. *Securing Letters When Possible*

There should be large co-operation among pastors and churches looking to the conservation of inactive or absentee members, in an endeavor to have such persons call for their letters and go into the fellowship of a sister church without unnecessary delay.

The practice which has grown up in the past few years of receiving applicants for church membership on a statement of their Christian experience, without making an effort to secure proper letters of dismission, is one which works harm to the churches, first by reason of the lowered respect for the church from which such a member comes, and secondly by causing members to be carried on two rolls. Persons who have lost fellowship ought to be led to be reinstated and come out by a proper letter.

A rural pastor in an adjoining state told the author that he had some twenty members living in Baltimore. He generously furnished their names and addresses. These were given to local pastors according to location. It was found that in practically every case the person visited had already joined a city church on Christian experience without even trying to secure a church letter.

3. *Keeping the Covenant Alive*

Church covenants usually include the following language: We moreover covenant together "that when we remove from this place, we will as soon as possible unite with some other church, where we can carry out the spirit of this covenant, and the principles of God's Word."

With large numbers of our people this covenant obligation is a dead letter. A young preacher called on a woman to ask her to join his church, as she lived near by. She blandly responded that she had been a member of a certain church fifteen years and was perfectly satisfied with her church relationship, yet the pastor discovered that she had not attended her church for years.

It had not occurred to her that church membership carried with it any responsibility.

SUGGESTIONS FOR FURTHER STUDY AND DISCUSSION

1. The frequency of observance of the Lord's Supper.
2. Present-day conformity to the world.
3. The work of deacons or a spiritual committee in disciplining a member.

Outline

Introduction

I. Constructive Discipline
1. Care in Receiving Members
2. Participation at the Lord's Supper
3. Immediate Enlistment

II. Self-Discipline
1. Personal Efforts
2. Overcoming Temptation
3. Courage and Faith
4. Pressing Toward the Goal
5. Simple Living
6. Willingness to Be Different
7. One's Interests the Test

III. Corrective Discipline
1. A Grave Problem
2. Overcoming Evil with Good
3. Noncontributing Members

IV. Punitive Discipline
1. Exclusion for Cause
2. Converting the Sinner
3. A Great Fault

V. Discipline by Erasure
1. Effort to Arouse Interest
2. Securing Letters When Possible
3. Keeping the Covenant Alive

CHAPTER VI

GROWTH IN WORLD MISSIONARY VISION

Jesus Christ is the Saviour of the world. "Neither is there any other name under heaven, that is given among men, wherein we must be saved" (Acts 4: 12 ASV). Jesus said, "The field is the world" (Matt. 13: 38). The growing Christian will, therefore, be interested in the spread of the gospel in all parts of the world, beginning where he lives but not stopping there.

When one considers the many unscriptural cults, the many millions of unsaved people in our own country, and the religions practiced in other nations, he is bound to conclude that Christ is needed everywhere, and to be glad of the gospel we profess. Paul said, "I am not ashamed of the gospel: for it is the power of God unto salvation to every one that believeth; to the Jew first, and also to the Greek" (Rom. 1: 16 ASV). The Christian faith is universal in its application, and gratitude should move every Christian to say:

> Can we whose souls are lighted
> With wisdom from on high;
> Can we to souls benighted
> The lamp of life deny?
>
> —UNKNOWN

I. MISSIONS IN THE BIBLE

1. *In the Old Testament*

Deeply embedded in the Old Testament is the purpose of God to redeem men of all nations. To Abram God said, "I will bless thee, and make thy name great; . . .

and in thee shall all families of the earth be blessed"
(Gen. 12: 2-3).

In Solomon's prayer at the dedication of the Temple
he said, "Moreover concerning the foreigner, that is not
of thy people Israel, when he shall come from a far
country for thy great name's sake, and thy mighty hand,
and thine outstretched arm; when they shall come and
pray toward this house: then hear thou from heaven, even
from thy dwelling-place, and do according to all that the
foreigner calleth to thee for; that all the peoples of the
earth may know thy name, and fear thee, as doth thy
people Israel" (2 Chron. 6: 32-33 ASV).

Isaiah prophesied, "Lo, these shall come from far; and,
lo, these from the north and from the west; and these
from the land of Sinim" (Isa. 49: 12 ASV). Of Jehovah's
house he said, "My house shall be called a house of
prayer for all peoples" (Isa. 56: 7 ASV).

Jehovah said to Jonah, "Should not I have regard
for Nineveh, that great city, wherein are more than six-
score thousand persons that cannot discern between their
right hand and their left hand?" (Jonah 4: 11).

The psalms are permeated with the missionary spirit.

Malachi wrote: "For from the rising of the sun even
unto the going down of the same my name shall be great
among the Gentiles" (Mal. 1: 11). Surely the Old Testament is a missionary book.

2. *In the New Testament*

When Jesus was born in Bethlehem an angel of the
Lord stood by the shepherds in the field and said, "Be
not afraid; for behold, I bring you good tidings of great
joy which shall be to all the people" (Luke 2: 10 ASV).

Christ's commission to his disciples is explicit, "Go ye
therefore, and make disciples of all the nations" (Matt.
28: 19 ASV).

During our Lord's public ministry he showed his great
interest in the Gentiles. Witness his dealings with the
Syrophenician woman (see Mark 7: 24-30) and the parable of the good Samaritan (Luke 10: 25-37).

Luke records the promise of power given by Jesus. "But ye shall receive power, when the Holy Spirit is come upon you: and ye shall be my witnesses both in Jerusalem, and in all Judaea and Samaria, and unto the uttermost part of the earth" (Acts 1: 8 ASV). The promise was fulfilled at Pentecost (Acts 2).

Because of the persecution that arose after the stoning of Stephen the disciples were "scattered abroad throughout the regions of Judaea and Samaria, except the apostles" (Acts 8: 1).

"In order that the strategy of Pentecost might be carried out it was necessary for the church to be scattered abroad. Those at Pentecost, hailing from every nation under heaven must go back to their homes and witness." (RAY).

When Christ appeared to Saul on the way to Damascus he said to him, "I appeared unto thee, to appoint thee a minister and a witness both of the things wherein thou hast seen me, and of the things wherein I will appear unto thee; delivering thee from the people, and from the Gentiles, unto whom I send thee, to open their eyes, that they may turn from darkness to light" (Acts 26: 16-18 ASV).

Philip proclaimed the glad tidings to the Samaritans as did Peter and John, who were sent to them by the apostles at Jerusalem. (See Acts 8: 14, 17, 25.)

Consider Peter's conclusion after he visited Cornelius at Caesarea following his vision on the housetop: "Of a truth I perceive that God is no respecter of persons: but in every nation he that feareth him and worketh righteousness, is acceptable to him" (Acts 10: 34-35 ASV). Disciples from Cyprus and Cyrene also preached Christ to the Greeks at Antioch. "And the hand of the Lord was with them: and a great number that believed turned unto the Lord," and when "the report concerning them came to the ears of the church which was in Jerusalem: and they sent forth Barnabas as far as Antioch: who, when he was come, and had seen the grace of God, was glad" (Acts 11:21-23 ASV).

On Paul's second missionary journey a man of Macedonia beckoned him to regions yet untouched and God turned the tide of evangelization westward into Europe, the cradle of modern civilization. Paul himself, in a career that knows no parallel in missionary annals, eventually reached Italy and probably Spain.

"On the basis of all the data available it has been estimated that by the close of the apostolic period the total number of Christians in the world had reached a half million" (GLOVER).

II. MISSIONS IN POST-APOSTOLIC CENTURIES

As stated by Dr. A. H. Newman in his *Manual of Church History*, "The Apostles had labored and died in spreading the gospel. Throughout Asia Minor, Greece, Italy, and possibly even farther west, the gospel had been preached and Christian churches established. Christianity had now to make its way without apostolic aid, in the face of obstacles that to human apprehension must have seemed well-nigh insuperable. In general we may characterize the present period as the period of gradual growth and the gradual corruption of Christianity, until it became strong enough on the one hand to make its adoption by the Empire a matter of policy and corrupt enough on the other to rejoice in such adoption."

1. *Proclamation of Constantine*

When in A.D. 312 Constantine proclaimed Christianity as the state religion, "A great injury was done to the cause of Christ, although it provided safety for Christians and liberty to preach. It brought into the state church large numbers of heathen people. Spiritual declension and loss of missionary zeal quickly followed" (GLOVER).

2. *The Work of Individuals*

As a protest against the state of affairs thus created, many devout men withdrew into solitude and undertook to evangelize the distant wilds. But there was a strong contrast between the evangelism of the early church and that of the period under review, in that it was the work of individuals rather than of organized Christianity.

"Usually the missionary would go among a people, carry with him some helpers and acquire land, a portion of which the community helpers would till for support and on which needed buildings would be erected. There was little support drawn from the home church. Sometimes support came from a state desiring to use the civilizing power of Christianity" (RAY).

3. *Failure of the Reformers*

The leaders of the Protestant Reformation seem to have had no serious sense of responsibility for missionary efforts in behalf of the heathen or Moslem peoples. Although they had a great conception of the fundamental doctrines of the evangelical faith, they showed remarkable ignorance of the scope of the divine plan and of Christian duty in relation to the gospel. However, it has been well said that the Reformation was perhaps responsible for the efforts of the Roman Church, which sought to make up its great losses to Protestantism in the old world by fresh conquests elsewhere.

(Today the Catholic Church, whose rapid growth in this country through the influx of foreign population was arrested by the immigration act which became effective in 1929, is carrying on a vigorous propaganda to win evangelical Christians, and especially Negroes, to their faith. The Catholic Evidence Guild is operating on street corners in our large cities much as the Salvation Army is accustomed to do.)

4. *Some Outstanding Missionaries*

During the period under review there were some outstanding missionaries, as Von Welz of Austria, who is credited with the first general appeal to the church; Spencer, who inaugurated the Pietist movement and led to the establishment of the University of Halle, which in turn gave birth to the first organized foreign missionary effort; Hans Egede, missionary to Greenland; Zinzendorf, who revived the Pietist movement in the Moravian church and whose motto was "I have one passion, it is He and He alone"; Christian Frederick Schwartz, of whom Dr. Ray says, "So fully appreciated were Schwartz's unselfish labors that when the English and the native governments reached an impasse in their negotiations the Rajah of Tanjore said, 'Send me the Christian. He will not deceive me.'"

III. MODERN MISSIONS

The modern missionary era began with William Carey in 1792, and he has been justly called "The Father of Modern Missions."

1. *Early American Missionaries*

Roger Williams, the founder of Rhode Island, was a missionary to the Indians in America, as were the Mayhews, five generations of whom labored effectively among the Indians of Massachusetts. David Brainerd also labored among the Indians near Cambridge, Massachusetts. "It was Brainerd's holy life that influenced Henry Martin to become a missionary and was the principal factor in William Carey's inspiration, who in turn moved Adoniram Judson" (GLOVER).

Viewing the subject of this chapter from the standpoint of American Baptists, we come first to Adoniram Judson and Luther Rice. In 1806 five students sat beneath the shelter of a haystack at Williamstown, Massachusetts, discussing the possibility of evangelizing the world. In 1810 Judson, with three others, including Luther Rice, offered himself for missionary work to the General Association of the Congregational Church. After being ordained he and his companions reached Calcutta in 1812. The denominational convictions of the Judsons were changed by the study of the New Testament and upon their arrival at Calcutta they were baptized. Luther Rice became a Baptist shortly after. They communicated with American Baptist leaders, and as a result the

Baptist Board of Foreign Missions was organized in 1814, principally for the purpose of providing support for Judson. And with that Board, operating in connection with the Triennial Convention, Southern Baptists affiliated.

2. *The Work of Luther Rice*

Luther Rice soon returned to the United States and spent the rest of his life helping the Baptists, North and South, to organize for effective missionary work. He was instrumental in the establishment of Columbian College in Washington, now known as George Washington University, and had much to do with the organization of district and state conventions, the founding of Baptist papers and many of our colleges along the Eastern seaboard. Sunday school work was carried on with vigor during that period and, as stated by Dr. Newman, the historian, "The introduction of so many innovations alarmed the ignorant and unprogressive elements of the denomination, and a large proportion of the Baptists of the South and Southwest zealously antagonized the missionary movement with all its accessories. Yet the party triumphed."

Even in Maryland, where in 1836 the churches suffered a split on account of differences relating to missionary co-operation, there had beeen a growing interest in missions. In 1818 the old Baltimore Baptist Association passed the following resolution: "That this association highly approves of measures adopted by the Board and fervently implores the abundant blessings of Jacob's God upon their every future effort to promote the interests of the Kingdom."

In 1819 the customary annual circular letter said: "To what short of the divine agency can we attribute the general missionary spirit which pervades Christians in both hemispheres?" The record also shows that those Baptists were encouraging "Domestic Missions" through an organization called the Domestic Missionary Society, of the Association.

3. *Beginning of the Southern Baptist Convention*

The Southern Baptist Convention was organized in 1845. Article II of the constitution says, "It shall be the design of the Convention to promote foreign and home missions, and other important objects connected with the Redeemer's Kingdom, and to combine for this purpose such portions of the Baptist denomination in the United States as may desire a general organization for Christian benevolence, which shall fully respect the independence and equal rights of the churches."

Immediately after the organization of the Convention two Boards were established, namely: the Board of Domestic Missions, then located at Marion, Alabama, and later moved to Atlanta, Georgia, and called the Home Mission Board; and the Foreign Mission Board, located then, as now, in Richmond, Virginia.

4. *Southern Baptist Missions*

If our vast constituency in the South is to be enlisted in the support of missions in accordance with the commission of our divine Lord, we must catch a vision of the opportunities for such work in connection with the missionary agencies in the several states and as set up by the Southern Baptist Convention. Let us, therefore, consider state missions, home missions, and foreign missions in order.

(1) *State Missions*

a. *A board in every state.*—Of fundamental importance to the missionary program is the work of state missions. In each of the eighteen states affiliated with the Southern Baptist Convention there is a state mission board, having its various departments of activity and established for the purpose of developing the churches in missionary spirit and practice.

b. *Functions enlarged.*—Prior to 1919, when the Baptist Seventy-Five Million Dollar Campaign was inaugurated, the state board majored on raising funds for work within the state and administering the evangelistic and cultural work committed to it by the state convention or general association. However, during the campaign, and subsequently under the Cooperative Program, the state organizations began generally to be used for the promotion of all the work fostered by the denomination.

c. *Qualifications of members.*—As stated by the late Dr. John T. Christian, in his introduction to the textbook *The Primacy of State Missions,* "The members of a state board should have a world outlook. The work is one. All missions are related and under the commands of the great commission no segregation is possible. Nothing less than worldwide evangelism and the Christian training and culture of all converts satisfy the demands of Jesus."

d. *Great importance of the state missions.*—The significance of state missions was well stated by the lamented Dr. A. V. Rowe in the book just mentioned: "The state mission appeal is in behalf of its own citizenship. It is employed first of all in supplying the destitution within the borders of the state; its hope and effort is to plant the gospel through the living ministry in country, in village, in town, and in city. . . . An intelligent state mission policy will build in a few years a denominational strength that will not only surprise but delight in its result in the state and will reach out its helpful hand to other states and nations that otherwise could never be reached."

No general board of the Southern Baptist Convention can effectively contact the vast constituency of our nineteen states and the District of Columbia, but this can be done by the state mission boards.

e. *The state, the unit of sovereignty.*—Dr. J. B. Gambrell, the great Baptist leader of a few years ago, wrote: "In America the state is the unit of sovereignty. The people of any given state have nearer relations with each other than with people in other states. Every state has its state feeling, a very proper thing and a very potential thing, when not carried too far. It is, therefore, most reasonable and has worked to the greatest benefit that in every state Baptists have perfected state organizations.

*Now out of print.

These state boards have a double purpose, first, to spread the gospel over that state, to knit up the forces of the state, to develop and conserve them; and in the second place, to turn all these forces on the wider fields beyond."

It has been well said that state missions is the "seed corn of the Kingdom."

f. *Fruits of state missions.*—A large proportion of the self-supporting churches in the South have been developed in co-operation with state mission boards and it has been observed that many of the churches thus aided are now among the most dependable bodies in co-operation with the denomination.

The present generation of members in these former mission churches will not know of the aid given by the state mission boards unless those responsible for their training tell them the facts. The author has had frequent occasion to review before such churches their early history in efforts to enlist them in better support of denominational causes. It has been interesting to note the surprise written on the faces of many making up the congregation. Sometimes it has been shown that more money was given by the state board for pastoral aid than the church had contributed to all benevolences over a long period of years.

The state mission boards must be enabled to continue giving aid to young and struggling churches or our people will not be able to give even fair support to the work of the general boards and other denominational enterprises.

g. *Department organization.*—In most of the southern states the work of the state mission board is conducted under both general and department leadership.

The state boards are composed of able men representing every district in the state, with a certain number of members living at, or near, headquarters to transact business between the sessions of the general board.

In all the states there is a Sunday school secretary and a Baptist Training Union secretary who labor under the general direction of the executive secretary. In a few cases Sunday school work and Baptist Training Union work are combined in one department.

In some of the states there is maintained a student department with a secretary who gives attention to Baptist students in schools and colleges.

The Woman's Missionary Union in each state is auxiliary to the state convention or general association, and the salary and expenses of the corresponding secretary and associates are paid either out of the funds allocated to state missions or the funds of the Cooperative Program before distribution.

(2) *Home Missions*

The Home Mission Board is now supporting several hundred missionaries and other workers. (See *Annual of Southern Baptist Convention* for exact figures.)

The Board is located in Atlanta, Georgia, and is composed of one or more members from each Southern state, with eighteen additional members living at or near the headquarters city. Its official staff consists of a president, vice-president, recording secretary, executive secretary-treasurer, and a corps of assistants.

The phases of mission work that must be provided for by the Board are numerous, and full consideration will convince open-minded Baptists of the important place that is held by the Board in its efforts to meet our denominational responsibility for the evangelization of the homeland, and for our work in Cuba, the Canal Zone, Panama, and Alaska.

a. Foreigners at our doors.—There are today approximately 9,000,000 belonging to the language groups. Only about 10 per cent of these are evangelized.

Therefore, the question faces Southern Baptists, What should be done to rescue the perishing in our Convention territory?

The Board is doing a large work among foreign peoples. Briefly stated, this includes activities among the following: the Spanish-speaking people in Texas, Oklahoma, Arizona, California, New Mexico, and Florida; the Chinese in San Antonio and El Paso, Texas, Phoenix, Arizona, Los Angeles and San Francisco, California, and Augusta, Georgia; the Russians in Los Angeles, California; the Japanese in Los Angeles, Richmond, and Sacramento, California; the Italians in Tampa, Florida, and Birmingham, Alabama; the French-speaking people of Louisiana and Texas. Work among foreign peoples includes our ministry through the Good Will Centers in the following cities: West Frankfort, Christopher, East St. Louis, and Granite City, Illinois, two at Baltimore, Maryland; Atlanta and Macon, Georgia. In fact, the missionaries in Illinois contact twenty-nine different nationalities. In California the Board also has an International Center in Berkeley.

b. Among the Indians.—The Board is serving among the Indians in Arizona, New Mexico, Oklahoma, Kansas, Mississippi, Alabama, North Carolina, and Florida. There are about 200 Indian Baptist churches, with 12,000 members. The Board is helping to support pastors, general missionaries, workers in Indian centers and Indian schools. We are also assisting worthy Indian youths to secure an education by means of scholarships.

c. The outposts.—The Board is working in Cuba, Panama, the Canal Zone, and Alaska.

There are approximately 80 churches and 142 missions in the four western provinces of Cuba served by Southern Baptists. These churches have a membership of 8,000 and 15,000 enrolled in Sunday school.

The Board has mission work among the West Indians, Anglos, and Panamanians in Panama and the Canal Zone. There are three Anglo churches, five West Indian (colored), and four Panamanian.

The Board's work in Alaska was started in 1948. It is now helping twelve workers and has helped to secure twelve pieces of property. Southern Baptists now have fifteen churches and nine mission stations in Alaska.

d. Among the deaf.—The Board's mission to the deaf is done by eight workers among 45,000 deaf in the entire Convention territory.

e. Among the Jews.—The Board has a Department of Jewish Work directed by its field secretary, Frank Halbeck. In addition to general promotion this department is co-operating with states in the establishment of Jewish departments of work in the cities.

f. Among the Negroes.—The Board operates Negro centers in twenty cities, and helps to support teachermissionaries in twenty-six Negro colleges. It also helps in Negro evangelistic work and Student Union work in Negro schools.

g. Migrant and ranch ministry.—There are approximately 750,000 migrants in the Convention territory. The Board now has three mobile units serving the three principal streams of migrants. They help to evangelize, and teach, and also assist the churches in areas visited by these migrants to minister to them while they are in their respective areas.

The Board has one missionary giving his entire time and attention to a ministry to the isolated ranchers in the West. This is an effort to reach people separated from our Baptist churches by long distances.

h. Co-operative mission work.—Through the Department of Co-operative Missions, the Board is serving in thirty-nine cities, thirteen of the rural states, and in all of the western states. Efforts are made to help establish new churches and support a trained ministry on new fields.

i. Evangelism.—The Board has a department of evangelism which is giving direction to simultaneous evangelistic efforts and is helping to support departments of evangelism in all the states desiring such assistance.

j. Other phases of work.—The Board employs about

360 students to serve in the Student Summer Mission Program.

The Chaplains' Commission endorses Southern Baptist chaplains for duty in our armed forces. About 425 are now in active service.

It also has departments of education and editorial service using the home mission magazine, mission study books, schools of missions, tracts, and visual aids in mission promotion.

There are two Baptist rescue missions in New Orleans, Louisiana. One is the Baptist Men's Rescue Mission. The other is the Woman's Emergency Home. In conjunction with the latter the Board has the Baptist Baby Home, an agency for placing babies.

(3) *Foreign Missions*

The Baptist who is earnestly working to bring the gospel to his local community, his state, and his nation will certainly be concerned for the salvation of souls in other lands. For this purpose Southern Baptists maintain the work of the Foreign Mission Board.

The Foreign Mission Board, organized in 1845, has headquarters in Richmond, Virginia. Members of the Board total 47, eighteen chosen from the vicinity of Richmond and the other 29 from the various states of the Southern Baptist Convention on the basis of Baptist population. The home office staff includes the executive secretary, the treasurer of the Board, the business manager, three regional secretaries—one for the Orient, one for Europe, Africa, and the Near East, and one for Latin America—a secretary for missionary personnel, and a secretary for education and promotion. Working in these departments are assistants to the heads of departments, director of visual education, book editor, research assistant, and editorial staff for the world journal, *The Commission*.

a. *Missionaries of the Board.* The first missionary of the Board was appointed September 1, 1845. He became the first in a succession of heroic Southern Baptists who were willing to invest their lives in the cause of world redemption. From the organization of the Board up to the close of 1953, it had sent out 1,904 missionaries. At the end of 1953 there were 908 missionaries in service and 134 emeritus missionaries.

b. *When missions were begun.*—The fields occupied by the missionaries and the dates on which they were opened are as follows: South China, 1846; Central China, 1847; Nigeria, 1850; North China, 1860; Italy, 1870; Mexico, 1880; South Brazil, 1881; North Brazil, 1882; Japan, 1889; Argentina, 1903; Interior China, 1904; Uruguay, 1911; Chile, 1917; Near East, 1920; Spain, Hungary, Yugoslavia, 1921; Hawaii, 1940; Colombia, 1941; Paraguay, 1945; Guatemala, Gold Coast, 1947; Venezuela, Costa Rica, Thailand, 1949; Ecuador, Formosa, Korea, Malaya, Peru, Philippines, Southern Rhodesia, 1950; Indonesia, 1951; Bahama Islands, 1952.

c. *Character of Work.*—The methods by which our foreign work is carried on include the operation of schools, academies, colleges, theological seminaries, and a university; hospitals, clinics, orphanages, field evangelism, publication societies, organization of Sunday schools, Training Unions, and W.M.U.'s, Bible distribution, etc. (*Note*—See the *Annual of the Southern Baptist Convention* for statistics concerning all our work in other lands.)

(4) *Woman's Missionary Union*

Woman's Missionary Union of the South was organized at Richmond, Virginia, in 1888. There is also a Woman's Missionary Union in each of the states co-operating with the Southern Baptist Convention.

The Lottie Moon Memorial Christmas offering for Foreign Missions and the Annie W. Armstrong offering for Home Missions have done much to strengthen the work of these boards. The societies major on support of the Cooperative Program in each state, the special

offerings being in addition to their efforts to enable the
churches to meet their regular apportionments for missions and other participating objects. The headquarters
of the Union are at Birmingham, Alabama, in charge of
a corresponding secretary and a staff of associates and
assistants.

SUGGESTIONS LOOKING TOWARD ENLARGED VISION

The following suggestions are made to Adult unions looking
toward the enlargement of the missionary vision of their members:

1. Color a state map, indicating the district associations, and
   mark thereon the mission churches.

2. Install a globe of the world, of sufficient size to be seen easily
   at any point in the meeting room.

3. Put up a missionary map of the world, marking thereon our
   Southern Baptist fields of labor.

4. Make a map of the Southern states, showing thereon the loca-
   tions of home mission fields.

5. Have accessible to the members the albums of the Foreign
   and Home Mission Boards showing the pictures of all the
   missionaries.

6. Conduct correspondence with selected missionaries in the
   state, home, and foreign fields.

7. Pray for the missionaries at home and abroad.

8. Use every opportunity to have a missionary speak to the
   union.

9. Magnify the missionary lessons published in the *Baptist Adult
   Union Quarterly.* Read our mission periodicals, *The Commission* and *Southern Baptist Home Missions.*

10. Encourage the members to read the tracts issued by the state,
    Home, and Foreign Boards, and to study the missionary
    books offered by the Sunday School Board, the Foreign
    Mission Board, and the Woman's Missionary Union.

OUTLINE

INTRODUCTION

I. MISSIONS IN THE BIBLE
   1. In the Old Testament
   2. In the New Testament

II. MISSIONS IN POST-APOSTOLIC CENTURIES
   1. Proclamation of Constantine
   2. The Work of Individuals
   3. Failure of the Reformers
   4. Some Outstanding Missionaries

III. MODERN MISSIONS
   1. Early American Missionaries
   2. The Work of Luther Rice
   3. Beginning of the Southern Baptist Convention
   4. Southern Baptist Missions
      (1) State Missions
         a. A board in every state
         b. Functions enlarged
         c. Qualifications of members
         d. Great importance of state missions
         e. The state, the unit of sovereignty
         f. Fruits of state missions
         g. Department organization
      (2) Home Missions
         a. Foreigners at our doors
         b. Among the Indians
         c. The outposts
         d. Among the deaf
         e. Among the Jews
         f. Among the Negroes
         g. Migrant and ranch ministry
         h. Co-operative mission work
         i. Evangelism
         j. Other phases of work
      (3) Foreign Missions
         a. Missionaries of the Board
         b. When missions were begun
         c. Character of work
      (4) Woman's Missionary Union

CHAPTER VII

GROWTH IN LOYALTY TO THE ETHICAL TEACHINGS OF JESUS

The growing Christian is at once confronted with the dictum of Jesus, "Except your righteousness shall exceed the righteousness of the scribes and Pharisees, ye shall in no case enter into the kingdom of heaven" (Matt. 5: 20). This must be so because of the very nature of his kingdom; as Paul states, "The kingdom of God is not eating and drinking, but righteousness and peace and joy in the Holy Spirit" (Rom. 14: 17 ASV). As we have already seen, justification is a term given to describe imputed righteousness while sanctification is progressive righteousness, or holiness of life.

"In the teachings of Jesus great emphasis is given to righteousness in the sense of inward purity. External righteousness, as of the scribes and Pharisees, is condemned as useless. Inward purity of heart, reaching to the motives and springs of action, is the Christian standard. The divine perfection, indeed, we must imitate. When Jesus says, 'Ye therefore shall be perfect, as your heavenly father is perfect' (Matt. 5: 48 ASV), he has special reference to the divine love. The entire Sermon on the Mount is an exposition of the righteousness of the kingdom" (*The Christian Religion in Its Doctrinal Expression*, p. 418).

Christians are to be more than others and they are to do more than others. William Secker, the author of a quaint book written in 1660, entitled *The Nonsuch Professor, builds this marvelous epigrammatic contribution to Christian living on the words of Jesus, "What do ye more than others?" (Matt. 5: 47). Said he, "The right-

*Out of print.

eous laws of God cannot connive at the unrighteous lives of men; they not only require truth without but within also."

Now it is clear that if we would follow a proper ethical standard it must come from the proper source. Good as may be some of the ethical teachings of other world religions, a Christian must follow the teachings of Christ. We live in a time when many moral standards that are offered are not founded on the teachings of our Lord, nor are they the just implications of the high principles enunciated by him. As the prophet exhorted, "To the law and to the testimony! if they speak not according to this word, surely there is no morning for them" (Isa. 8: 20 ASV). So Christians are always to inquire for light and guidance at the feet of Christ.

The ethical teachings of Jesus are found principally in the Sermon on the Mount. Consider some of them.

I. CHRIST'S TEACHING CONCERNING MURDER

1. The Law

"Ye have heard that it was said to them of old time, Thou shalt not kill; and whosoever shall kill shall be in danger of the judgment: but I say unto you, that every one who is angry with his brother shall be in danger of the judgment; and whosoever shall say to his brother, Raca, shall be in danger of the council; and whosoever shall say, Thou fool, shall be in danger of the hell of fire" (Matt. 5:21-22 ASV).

2. The Interpretation

The commandment against murder is well understood wherever Moses is read, but Christians must understand from the words of Jesus that God looks not alone upon the overt act, which to this day in most states of America is punishable by death, but also upon the heart, out of which such an overt act proceeds; that physical murder does not always occur by no means relieves those who entertain anger against a fellow man. It opposes itself to love, which is the essential principle of Christianity, and if allowed to reign within may lead to the overt act, for "out of it [the heart] are the issues of life" (Prov. 4:23).

"He is a murderer whose heart is full of hatred, though his hands be free from violence" (SECKER).

3. The Christian Way of Reconciliation

Jesus not only states his ethic on the subject of murder, but states the proper course for his followers, to wit, that "if therefore thou art offering thy gift at the altar, and there rememberest that thy brother hath ought against thee, leave there thy gift before the altar, and go thy way, first be reconciled to thy brother, and then come and offer thy gift" (Matt. 5: 23-24 ASV). It will be observed that the onus of responsibility for seeking reconciliation is on the one who has offended. If a Christian has caused another to be angered toward him, it is his duty to seek reconciliation. It is far more than to be willing to be reconciled. Reconciliation must be sought.

A good deacon became offended with a denominational executive because of a statement made in the heat of an associational address concerning the primitive Baptists. After many months, during which relations were strained in a most embarrassing degree, a letter from the executive to his offended brother, apologizing for any word that should not have been spoken and requesting a conference, resulted after forty-eight hours in complete reconciliation and understanding. That servant of the denomination has few better friends than the man who had been aggrieved by an utterance which was in no way personal.

II. CHRIST'S TEACHING CONCERNING ADULTERY

1. The Law

"Ye have heard that it was said, Thou shalt not commit adultery: but I say unto you, that every one that looketh on a woman to lust after her hath committed adultery with her already in his heart" (Matt. 5: 27-28 ASV).

2. *The Inner Motive*

Again Jesus gives emphasis to the motive of one's heart. All adulteries emanate from within. When David walked upon the roof of his house and saw Bathsheba he coveted Uriah's wife. He did not take her to be his wife until Uriah, placed in the front line of battle, had been slain, but Nathan the prophet, applying his parable of the one ewe lamb, said to David, "Thou art the man," and he confessed, "I have sinned against the Lord" (2 Sam. 12: 7, 13). The heart, through the eyes of the king, had led him into a crime against God and man. Jesus therefore admonishes: "If thy right eye causeth thee to stumble, pluck it out, and cast it from thee: for it is profitable for thee that one of thy members should perish, and not thy whole body be cast into hell" (Matt. 5:29 ASV).

3. *The Example of Adults*

The Christian who goes to places of amusement where he sees salacious pictures, or reads books which present the same in unholy words, thereby opens the way to commit adultery in his heart, if, indeed, he does not fall under condemnation for the act itself. The adult Christian has great responsibility for younger persons, who are apt to imitate their elders.

III. CHRIST'S TEACHING CONCERNING DIVORCE

1. *The Law*

"It was said also, Whosoever shall put away his wife, let him give her a writing of divorcement: but I say unto you, that every one that putteth away his wife, saving for the cause of fornication, maketh her an adulteress: and whosoever shall marry her when she is put away committeth adultery" (Matt. 5 31-32 ASV). "The righteous laws of God cannot connive at the unrighteous lives of men; therefore he that lusteth after and he that liveth with a woman, are both adulterers" (SECKER).

2. *The Scriptural Ground*

The granting of divorces on other than scriptural grounds, as just stated, has become one of the most hurtful practices in our own and other countries. It has become more and more easy to secure divorces, largely on the ground of incompatibility. Companionate marriages are advocated by some.

"The choice is a permanent one, and the union only becomes more close and sacred the longer it lasts. If to first love, as it is called, there attaches a beauty which has evoked the enthusiasm of poets and romancers, the love of old age is not less beautiful, when it has survived all the changes and chances of life only becoming mellower with the passing of the years" (*The Ethics of Jesus*, STALKER, p. 338).

3. *The Sanctity of Marriage*

The sanctity of the marriage vows has been broken down in many places. The papers reek with the publicity of such divorces. Some ministers of the gospel do not hesitate to marry divorced persons, without even inquiring as to the grounds of separation. As a result the normal family life of America has distinctly declined during the past several decades.

A prominent Presbyterian minister in a large city recently celebrated the thirtieth anniversary of his present pastorate. In reply to a reporter's question as to his attitude about marriage the minister said, "I never perform the ceremony unless I am personally acquainted with the pair seeking marriage." In a number of places in our country ordained ministers have prostituted their office by the commercialization of the authority to marry, especially so in Maryland where no one other than a preacher, priest, or rabbi may perform marriages.

Is the word of Jesus on divorce still binding? Jesus told the people of his day that Moses granted divorce only because of the hardness of their hearts. "Moses, for the hardness of the hearts of the people with whom

*Now out of print.

he had to deal—that is, to prevent worse from happening—afforded a means for putting away; and the same course has been followed by too complaisant governments in both ancient and modern times. But Jesus laid an arrest on this course; and, wherever his name is respected, his authority will savor opinion and legislation toward a purer standard" (*The Ethics of Jesus, STALKER, p. 340).

Today Christians need to ponder well Christ's words and put a strong curb upon this unholy business. Divorcees ought to be made to understand that if they propose to violate the ethics of Jesus, they must not expect his ministers to co-operate with them.

"There can, I think, be no reasonable doubt that Jesus made the marriage bond indissoluble.

"For this rigidity, so far as our sources of information tell us, he gave no reason except the quotation from Genesis 'And they shall be one flesh.' It seems to have been a part of his intuition of the will of God. But we must read his words in the light of his attitude to women and children, which is markedly different from anything else found in the world. It is undoubtedly this intuitive sense of the essential worth of all women and children that lay beneath his prohibition of divorce. For it is on the woman as childbearer that the heaviest burden entailed by irregular sexual unions necessarily falls—at least when these relations lead to offspring and when society rests on the family, as in the most advanced civilizations it has so far done. In such a society it is only where marital fidelity is preserved that children are given a fair chance of development. The teaching of Jesus on marriage and the family is of one piece with his whole outlook on life" (*Christianity as Life).

IV. CHRIST'S TEACHING CONCERNING PROFANITY

1. *The Law*

"Again, ye have heard that it was said to them of old time, Thou shalt not forswear thyself, but shalt per-

*Now out of print.

form unto the Lord thine oaths: but I say unto you, Swear not at all; . . . but let your speech be, Yea, yea; Nay, nay: and whatsoever is more than these is of the evil one" (Matt. 5: 33-37 ASV). Profanity is forbidden in the Third Commandment: "Thou shalt not take the name of the Lord thy God in vain! for the Lord will not hold him guiltless that taketh his name in vain" (Ex. 20: 7).

2. The Legal Oath

Our Lord is not here condemning legal oaths. Christians do no wrong when they take such oaths as are required by the state.

3. The Practice of Swearing

The profane use, in conversation, of the names by which we know the deity, which has through the ages been prevalent, is a thing which every Christian should avoid. It is useless as well as sinful. This habit, with many, is not meant to be a profanation of God, but nevertheless it is displeasing to God and is weakening to moral character. Profanity adds no strength to a man's words but rather raises a suspicion against the truthfulness of the one using them.

"Recognized probity is the surest of all oaths" (MADAM NECKER).

V. CHRIST'S TEACHING CONCERNING NONRESISTANCE

1. The Law

"Ye have heard that it was said, An eye for an eye, and a tooth for a tooth: but I say unto you, Resist not him that is evil: but whosoever smiteth thee on thy right cheek, turn to him the other also. And if any man would go to law with thee, and take away thy coat, let him have thy cloak also. And whosoever shall compel thee to go one mile, go with him two. Give to him that asketh thee, and from him that would borrow of thee turn not thou away" (Matt. 5: 38-42 ASV).

2. *The Need for Self-Control*

This is the King's law of nonresistance. It must not be refused because it goes against one's grain. It is not natural to act that way, but it is Christian. The person who practices such self-control and patience as is here taught will unquestionably strengthen his own Christian character. The temptation to regard it as too ideal has robbed many a man of great spiritual blessings.

A Christian must not be too sensitive to wrongs done toward him, but must be long-suffering toward those who have not the spirit of Christ.

3. *The Teaching of Paul*

Paul admonished the Corinthians: "Dare any of you, having a matter against his neighbor, go to law before the unrighteous, and not before the saints? . . . already it is altogether a defect in you, that ye have lawsuits one with another. Why not rather take wrong? why not rather be defrauded?" (1 Cor. 6: 1, 7 ASV).

VI. CHRIST'S TEACHING CONCERNING LOVE OF ENEMIES

1. *The Law*

"Ye have heard that it was said, Thou shalt love thy neighbor, and hate thine enemy: but I say unto you, Love your enemies, and pray for them that persecute you; that ye may be sons of your Father who is in heaven" (Matt. 5: 43-45 ASV). In other words, our enemy is our neighbor though he may not act like one. When Jesus was reviled he reviled not again, but said, "Father, forgive them; for they know not what they do" (ASV). As William Secker says, "As an echo returns the voice it receives, so many will show kindness where kindness is shown, but shall publicans be as godly as the Lord's disciples? Shall the sons of men equalize the sons of God? Shall the law of nature swell to so high a tide as the law of grace? This were for the dribbling rivulet to vie with the drowning ocean; this were for royalty to degenerate into beggary; and for the meridian sun to yield no more light than the shades" (*The Nonsuch Professor).

2. The Teaching of the Apostles

Now the apostles have much to say about Christian ethics. An examination of the epistles makes it clear that they followed closely the teachings of Christ. We should remember that the apostles wrote by inspiration of the Holy Spirit who was promised by Jesus to bring all things to their remembrance and guide them into all truth.

Some Bible critics would discriminate between the sayings of Jesus and the teachings of his apostles, but such discriminations are not warranted, if we accept the authority of Scripture.

Paul does not excuse the Gentiles, the heathen of his day, for their sinful practices, even though they were not governed by the written law. He concludes that they are morally responsible when he says:

"For when Gentiles that have not the law do by nature the things of the law, these, not having the law, are the law unto themselves; in that they show the work of the law written in their hearts, their conscience bearing witness therewith, and their thoughts one with another accusing or else excusing them; in the day when God shall judge the secrets of men, according to my gospel, by Jesus Christ" (Rom. 2: 14-16 ASV).

Because these epistles were written for the edification of Christians the responsibility even of the heathen should cause us to consider the standards given by Christ and his apostles, for as William Secker says, "Superabundance of privilege demands superabundance of practice."

---

*Out of print.

Paul admonishes the Roman Christian to "abhor that which is evil" (Rom. 12: 9), and like his Master, he tells them to "render to no man evil for evil" (ASV); to seek to live at peace with all men; to "avenge not yourselves," and to feed and give drink to one's enemies, all these exhortations being based on "the expulsive power of a new affection," as Thomas Chalmers interpreted the words of Paul, "Be not overcome of evil, but overcome evil with good" (Rom. 12: 21).

Paul reminds the Corinthian Christians that while some of them had aforetime been guilty of gross sins, as fornication, adultery, theft, coveteousness, drunkenness, and extortion, they had been washed, sanctified, justified in the name of the Lord Jesus Christ (see 1 Cor. 6: 11).

To the end that Christians might not fall into the sinful practices he had named, they were admonished to regard their bodies as the temples of the Holy Spirit: "Ye are not your own; for ye were bought with a price: glorify God therefore in your body" (1 Cor. 6:19-20 ASV). He also exhorts the Ephesians to be "imitators of God, . . . and walk in love, even as Christ also loved you, and gave himself up for us, an offering and a sacrifice to God for an odor of a sweet smell" (Eph. 5: 1-2 ASV): and goes on to say that fornication and uncleanness, or coveteousness, must not even be named among them; "nor filthiness, nor foolish talking, or jesting." Christians are not to be partakers with them for the reason that they who "were once darkness" are now "light in the Lord" (ASV).

On the basis of the new life in Christ, the apostle argues that the Colossian believers are to "seek those things which are above" (Col. 3: 1), and admonishes them to "Put to death therefore your members which are upon the earth: fornication, uncleanness, passion, evil desire, and covetousness, which is idolatry"; and put away "anger, wrath, malice, railing, shameful speaking out of your mouth: lie not one to another; seeing that ye have put off the old man with his doings, and have put on the new man, that is being renewed unto knowledge after the image of him that created him" (Col. 3: 5, 8-10 ASV).

Wives are to honor their husbands, husbands are to love their wives, children are to obey their parents, servants are to obey their masters, and masters are to be just in their dealings with their servants. (See Col. 3: 18-25).

Peter deals in essence with the same ethical teachings, as does James who concludes his exhortation by saying that the Christian is to "keep himself unspotted from the world."

3. *The Bane of Present-Day Living*

The growing Christian should so study the moral and social teachings of Jesus and the apostles, with their implications, as to learn the will of God for the individual life, knowing that he is to be not only a professor of faith in Christ but also a doer of the Word for he said, "Ye therefore shall be perfect, as your heavenly Father is perfect" (Matt. 5:48 ASV).

The bane of present-day living, even among professed Christians, is the tendency to accept the ideals of the Jesus way of life in only an academic sense, failing to make these ideals liquid, thus setting before the world an example of holy living.

SUGGESTIONS FOR FURTHER STUDY AND DISCUSSION

1. What are the fundamental causes of the American divorce problem? (*Note*—The teacher should ask one or more members of the class to study this problem and bring a brief report to the class. Statistics are available in public libraries.) What can church members do about it?

2. Should Christ's teaching concerning nonresistance be extended to international relations? If so, how?

CHAPTER VIII

GROWTH IN CHRISTIAN CITIZENSHIP

Christians are citizens of two worlds. They are first members of the kingdom of God. In Moffatt's Translation Christians are spoken of as "a colony of heaven" (Phil. 3: 20). They are to "seek first his kingdom" (Matt. 6: 33). They are to confess that they are strangers and pilgrims on the earth. (See Heb. 11: 13.) They are to be "a people for his own possession, zealous of good works" (Titus 2: 14 ASV), and they are also instructed to deny ungodliness and worldly lusts and to live soberly and righteously and godly in this present world. (See Titus 2: 12.)

Christians are declared by Jesus to be "the salt of the earth" and "the light of the world" (See Matt. 5: 13-14.)

I. THE CHRISTIAN AND THE STATE

1. *Liberty and Tolerance*

The Constitution of the United States guarantees to its citizens full civil and religious liberty for which boon we have to thank our Baptist forebears, beginning with Roger Williams, who led in the establishment, in 1643, in Rhode Island, of the first colony (state) in which there was a complete liberty of conscience both for Gentile and Jew.

That such provision was made first in Maryland cannot be proved. Religious "toleration" among Christians was as far as Lord Baltimore went. Roger Williams' contribution to religious liberty antedated the toleration act of the Maryland Legislature several years, and under the beneficial laws of Rhode Island even an atheist was given full freedom of conscience.

The Maryland Act of 1649 reads, "That no persons professing to believe in Jesus Christ shall be molested in respect of their religion, or the free exercise thereof, or be compelled to the belief or practice of any other religion, against their consent, so that they be not unfaithful to the proprietary, or conspire against the civil government. That persons molesting any other in respect of his religious tenets shall pay treble damages to the party aggrieved and twenty shillings to the proprietary. That the reproaching of any with opprobrious epithets of religious distinctions shall forfeit ten shillings to the person aggrieved. That any one speaking reproachfully against the Blessed Virgin or the Apostles shall forfeit five pounds, but blasphemy against God shall be punished with death."

2. *Church and State Separate*

Our Federal Constitution also provides for the complete separation of church and state.

"Historians ascribe to the Baptists the chief credit for the establishment of this principle in the United States" (*The People Called Baptists*, McDANIEL).

Dr. A. T. Robertson well says in his postwar book, **The New Citizenship:* "In having a churchless state, as is right, we have secured a godless state, which is wrong. The state cannot do without God any more than the individual can. Not that God need be in the Constitution or on our coins, though there is no harm in that. What the state needs is not a statute god (Germany has that) nor a state god (the Roman Empire had that). What the state must do is to lay the foundation in righteousness that alone exalts a nation. Nothing else will stand."

As Dr. P. T. Forsythe says, "A nation is Christian not when a church is established by law, but when righteousness is established by conscience within its workers."

*Now out of print.

Paul exhorts Christians, "Let every soul be in subjection to the higher powers: for there is no power but of God: and the powers that be are ordained of God. Therefore he that resisteth the power, withstandeth the ordinance of God: and they that withstand shall receive to themselves judgment" (Rom. 13: 1-2 ASV).

In those countries where the church is supported by the state, there is not such religious freedom as we enjoy in America. Besides, paternalism is not a real help to the church, failing as it does to develop its members in self-support. It is manifest that where ministers of the gospel depend upon the government for support, they cannot be independent of the state, free to speak their message without regard to those who may be affected thereby.

3. *Christian Conscience*

The question of how far the state may go in asserting power over the conscience is difficult. It requires great wisdom as well as great courage to know and to do what is right. As Dr. Robertson says, "What if conscience and the state conflict? Then the conscience should see to it that it is right. It may need fresh light. If, after all is said and done, the conscience stands its ground, that is each man's privilege. Only a man must be willing to pay the price for such a stand with his life if need be. This is what Jesus did. This is what Peter and John stood ready to do: "Whether it is right in the sight of God to hearken unto you rather than unto God, judge ye: for we cannot but speak the things which we saw and heard" (Acts 4: 19-20 ASV). And yet Peter wrote: "Honour all men. Love the brotherhood. Fear God. Honour the king" (1 Peter 2: 17).

Paul exhorted that "supplications, prayers, intercessions, thanksgivings, be made for all men; for kings and all that are in high place; that we may lead a tranquil and quiet life in all godliness and gravity" (1 Tim. 2: 1-2 ASV).

II. The Christian and Taxation

1. *The Teaching of Jesus*

The state must of necessity levy taxes on property and incomes to meet the expenses of administering justice, international relations, protection for our nationals on land and on sea, old-age pensions, public education, general relief, and all proper governmental functions, whether local, state, or national. The Christian citizen should not seek to evade such assessments. It is not right that one person should be relieved of the burdens of state at the expense of his fellow citizens.

When Jesus said to the disciples of the Pharisees in answer to the question "Is it lawful to give tribute to Caesar?": "Render therefore unto Caesar the things which are Caesar's; and unto God the things that are God's" (Matt. 22:21), Caesar claimed to be God. The emperor-cult was the chief religion of the empire. Benjamin Franklin said: "The taxes are indeed very heavy, and if those laid by the government were the only ones we pay, we might more easily discharge them; but we have many others and much more grievous to many of us. We are taxed twice as much for our idleness, three times as much for our pride and four times as much for our folly; and from these taxes the commissioners cannot ease or deliver us by allowing an abatement."

2. *The Cost of Crime*

The Federal Bureau of Investigation estimates the annual cost of crime in the United States at not less than fifteen billion dollars. This is about ten times the amount spent for all church work in a year.

(1) *The Extent of Crime.*—The following facts from *Uniform Crime Reports*, January, 1950, tell a graphic story:

In 1949 crime in the United States totaled an estimated

1,763,290 serious offenses, a crime every 18 seconds. During an average day, 293 persons were feloniously killed or assaulted; 162 robberies were committed; more than 1,100 places burglarized; over 440 cars were stolen, in addition to 2,800 other thefts.

Crime was up 4.5 per cent across the nation during 1949 compared with the previous year.

(2) *Prison Conditions.*—According to the Osborne Association, there are six deplorable conditions connected with prison life in America, as follows:

a. Lack of facilities to segregate certain classes of offenders.

b. Overcrowding at most prisons.

c. Poor living conditions.

d. Inadequate medical facilities.

e. Ineffective disciplinary methods.

f. Defective and inadequate parole facilities and methods.

(3) *Church Attendance and Crime.*—Of 460 youths sentenced to the Massachusetts Reformatory, 421 (91.5%) never attended church.

Should the state levy a tax for a purpose the payment of which would violate the Christian's conscience, instructed by the Word of God, as England did a few years ago when Parliament passed the education bill, whereby nonconformists were required to support priestly and popish teaching in the public schools, it would be proper for a conscientious objector to protest such a law by refusal to pay, as was done by John Clifford, the great Baptist leader of that day, Sir George White and others, and if necessary to suffer the confiscation of property. Ministers and laymen went to jail and suffered distraint of their goods, which were seized by the sheriff, rather than pay the stipend for ecclesiastical tyranny.

3. *The Action of the Southern Baptist Convention*

The Southern Baptist Convention, in session at Memphis, Tennessee, in May, 1935, unanimously adopted the following resolution:

(1) "That we hereby reaffirm our devotion to the fundamental New Testament doctrine and fundamental principle of the American government, the separation of church and state; religion must be kept free from all entangling alliances with government and government must not assume patronage, sponsorship or control over religion in any form.

(2) "That we also declare it to be our abiding conviction that this fundamental doctrine of the New Testament and sacred principle of government cannot be maintained if and when the government becomes the financial sponsor for churches, provides financial subsidies for churches or other religious institutions, or appropriates money out of the public treasury to sectarian institutions.

(3) "That we would call the attention of Southern Baptist pastors and churches to these matters and would urge them with all diligence to maintain this doctrine in all of their activities and relationships and at all costs to abstain from borrowing money from the government, receiving the financial endorsement of the government and receiving appropriations of funds from the public treasury, whether national or state.

(4) "That we would enter our earnest protest against the violation of this principle by any Baptist church or Baptist institution or by others, and especially against the appropriation or application of public funds to sectarian institutions of whatever name or order."

No seminary or other institution owned or fostered by the Southern Baptist Convention received aid from the Federal Government for their students during the depression, notwithstanding the widespread use of such funds by others. Thus Southern Baptists may consistently stand for the principle of complete separation of church and state. The Southern Baptist Convention in 1937 reaffirmed its action of 1935 in resolutions.

III. The Christian and the Franchise

1. *Responsibility of Citizenship*

In our country we have a democracy in which each citizen has responsibility for the conduct of the government. The people are really the government. If the administration of county, city, state or national government is not wisely and honestly done, the remedy is ultimately in the hands of the people. "The Christian cannot escape his duties as a citizen. He has no right to shirk them or resign them to others, not even to the city 'boss' or to the party machine. The Christian can get no sympathy from Christ for leaving the affairs of state to selfish and evil men. Christians have too often been too cowardly and careless. They have followed the lead of the party 'boss' without regard to the ethical aspects of the issues at stake. The Christian must take Christ to the polls in no pharisaical sense, free from all cant, with the utmost courage and determination" (**The New Citizenship*).

2. *Influence of Church Members*

America is spoken of as a Christian nation; yet with a population of 150,697,361 in 1950 only about 85,705,-280 are definitely identified with any religious body. Taking no account of the children who are not yet eligible to membership, there are still at least 40,000,000 responsible persons who are not actually members of churches or synagogues. But if all the church members of legal age would do their duty in the matter of exercising the franchise, great improvements would be made by the political parties in the whole business of government.

*Now out of print.

3. *Women and the Vote*

In 1920 the women of America were given the right to vote. It was then assumed that the women, the home-makers of the country, would, generally speaking, put their immense power and influence behind every right-eous cause. It is now realized that this was a false as-sumption, as shown by the attitude of thousands of women toward such a moral question as the repeal of the Eighteenth Amendment. Many women, along with many men, placed party loyalty above principle, and thus the prohibition of the sale of intoxicants as a bev-erage was set aside so far as the Constitution was con-cerned; and although both of the great parties had said in their platforms that there must be no return of the saloon, the terrible curse of liquor has returned in very large degree. When Christians are ready to do their duty as citizens we shall again see our country rid of this wicked business.

A Government inspector, after much observation and experience, recently said, "Liquor men are not law-abid-ing citizens." While there is nothing new about that statement, it shows that the liquor dealers did not learn anything during the period of prohibition.

IV. THE CHRISTIAN AND POLITICS

1. *Politics and Statesmanship*

There is in actual practice a difference between poli-tics and statesmanship but that should not be so. Both politics and statesmanship are defined as the science of government but a politician is defined as "one who seeks to subserve the interests of a political party merely."

"The worth of a state, in the long run, is the worth of the individuals composing it" (J. STUART MILL).

2. *The Christian and Politics*

Many a good man stays out of politics because of the company he thinks he must keep. We have had and still have many God-fearing and honorable men and women in the field of politics, and their influence is far greater than their number might suggest. Our greatest Presidents have been earnest Christians, men who believed in providence and prayer.

3. *Examples of Great Christian Leaders*

George Washington, Abraham Lincoln, Woodrow Wilson and others besought God for guidance and strength in the hour of national crisis. Jefferson Davis, Stonewall Jackson, Robert E. Lee and other leaders of the Southern Confederacy were devout Christians. In the South today a majority of the governors are Christians. This is also true of our congressmen and senators.

V. The Christian and the Social Order

1. *Social Responsibility*

It is unreasonable to think of a growing Christian who does not influence for good the social order of which he is inextricably a part. When the Christian life is lived in right relation to God and in co-operation with kindred souls, there is fostered an age of interclass, interracial, and international goodwill. "None of us liveth to himself, and none dieth to himself" (Rom. 14: 7).

Modern means of transportation and communication have made the whole world a neighborhood, so that more and more men are involved with the rest of mankind. What happens anywhere today is immediately broadcast to all who are "listening in."

The so-called "social gospel" is really a misnomer, for there is only one gospel and that is a gospel of individual salvation through the meritorious work of Jesus Christ, but all Christians are members of God's family and in such relationship there are social responsibilities which cannot be avoided by those who would live obedient lives.

2. The "Abundant Life"

Much is being said and written today concerning the "abundant life" by which, from the standpoint of the state, is meant the necessities of life, education, and culture for all the people. When Jesus said: "I came that they may have life, and may have it abundantly" (John 10: 10), he was speaking of the spiritual life which he came to bestow, but certainly such a life has its implications for all the life of a Christian. As previous chapters undertook to show, spiritual life must have a beginning, must be developed and must be expressed. It is the author's view that the Christian will express his life in all the ways that make for a better world. "For the grace of God hath appeared, bringing salvation to all men, instructing us, to the intent that, denying ungodliness and worldly lusts, we should live soberly and righteously and godly in this present world; looking for the blessed hope and appearing of the glory of the great God and our Saviour Jesus Christ" (Titus 2: 11-13).

Fulness of life means living together as a family of individuals, as groups, as nations. The Christian pattern calls for these things which make such a life possible—goodwill, forbearance, mutual trust, mutual respect, mutual love.

3. True Nationalism

Today's world is permeated with that kind of nationalism which leads to war and chaos. Such nationalism thinks in terms of self and does not regard the interests of others. There is, however, the right kind of nationalism, and only with it as a foundation can we build a true internationalism.

Basil Mathews says: "Our task is to re-create our nation as it is into the nation that God wills it to be, so that it can offer its own special gift to the world of nations. This is the true foundation of internationalism, which is far greater than any supercilious cosmopolitanism that has no loyalty to mankind as a whole because it has none to home and nation. Our ultimate loyalty is a spiritual one, to the kingdom of God; but that loyalty must begin to be incarnate and concrete and passionate in the home and the nation before it can be real in relation to mankind" (*World Tides in the Far East, p. 138).

The study of Christian missions has broadened the outlook of many and prepared them to recognize the contribution they are to make to the people of those nations among whom our missionaries are laboring. Our country has no territorial designs or objectives toward other nations. The present national administration has properly emphasized the need of our having toward other countries, the strong and the weak, an attitude of neighborliness. That attitude is according to the Christian principle of love to our neighbors as stated by Jesus Christ, who said, "Thou shalt love thy neighbor as thyself." In such a matter our government is really controlled by the crystallized public sentiment of the people who make up our country. If the Christian part of our population will definitely stand for goodwill toward other nations, our government will find it easier to put into effect the proper concrete expressions of that sentiment.

The members of the Adult union have frequent occasion to help in the creation of sentiments of goodwill toward mankind. Only when this is done, our members should see to it that the principles for which we stand shall find their way, through us, to those who represent us in Congress. This is not to mix the church with the state in a wrong way, but Baptists have always held to the right of petition and protest and sometimes they have done the courteous thing of commending those in authority for doing the things that we consider right.

For example, the Baltimore Association, in 1808, wrote as follows, in part, to President Thomas Jefferson:

---

*Out of print.

In correspondence with a practice which appears consonant with propriety and justice, we embrace this opportunity of expressing our sense of your numerous and important services in the cause of civil and religious liberty, and in promoting the welfare and happiness of the people of the United States. In reviewing the acts of your public life, our minds are forcibly impressed with the recollection that you were the author of the Declaration of Independence; an instrument in which we recognize the vindication of our rights, the declaration of our wrongs, and the objects for which government is instituted.

.   .   .   .

We consider it proper, in the capacity of a religious body, to express our feelings of gratitude, and sentiments of approbation, for your exercises and services in behalf of religious liberty within your own state. The friends of piety must ever remember that the act passed by the Virginia legislature in 1786, for the establishment of religious freedom, emanated from you.

On retiring from the high station, which you have filled with so much dignity and credit to yourself and advantage to our country, it is proper for us to express our approbation of the reasons which influence you to this determination.

(Signed) OBADIAH B. BROWN, Moderator
JOHN WELCH, Clerk

The following gracious reply was received:

I receive with great pleasure the friendly address of the Baltimore Baptist Association, and am sensible how much I am indebted to the kind disposition which dictated it.

In our early struggles for liberty, religious freedom could not fail to become a primary object; all men felt the right, and a just animation to obtain it was excited in all. I was one only among the many who befriended its establishment, and am entitled but in common with others to a proportion of that approbation which follows the fulfilment of a duty.

.   .   .   .

I am happy in your approbation of my reasons for determining to retire from a station in which the favor of my fellow-citizens has so long continued and supported me: and I return your kind prayers with supplications to the same Almighty Being for your future welfare and that of our beloved country.

(Signed) TH. JEFFERSON

VI. THE CHRISTIAN AND PATRIOTISM

1. *Patriotism Defined*

Patriotism is love of country. It is next to the love of God. It was a Baptist who wrote our national hymn, "My Country, 'Tis of Thee." Baptists have proved their patriotism and loyalty not alone in times of peace but in times of conflict as well.

2. *Patriotism and the Presidency*

The presidential office should be respected. We may differ in politics and as we may not care personally for the man who fills the presidential chair, but it ill becomes Christians to speak discourteously of the President. Paul exhorted Timothy to make "supplications, prayers, intercessions . . . for kings, and for all that are in authority."

"Of the whole sum of life no small part is that which consists of a man's relation to his country and his feelings concerning it" (GLADSTONE).

3. *Patriotism and the Supreme Court*

Every Baptist, who can do so, should avail himself of the privilege of looking in on the Supreme Court of the United States, one of the most dignified judicial bodies in the world. Our country is safe so long as the Supreme Court is held in the high esteem it merits from our people.

SUGGESTIONS FOR FURTHER STUDY AND DISCUSSION

1. Ask the members of the class to read the Constitution of the United States.
2. Contrast "freedom" in America with that in other nations.
3. What is the proper course of action for a Christian citizen with reference to laws which he feels are wrong?
4. Discuss the right of petition and protest.

OUTLINE

INTRODUCTION

I. THE CHRISTIAN AND THE STATE
   1. Liberty and Tolerance
   2. Church and State Separate
   3. Christian Conscience

II. THE CHRISTIAN AND TAXATION
   1. The Teaching of Jesus
   2. The Cost of Crime
   3. The Action of the Southern Baptist Convention

III. THE CHRISTIAN AND THE FRANCHISE
   1. Responsibility of Citizenship
   2. Influence of Church Members
   3. Women and the Vote

IV. THE CHRISTIAN AND POLITICS
   1. Politics and Statesmanship
   2. The Christian and Politics
   3. Examples of Great Christian Leaders

V. THE CHRISTIAN AND THE SOCIAL ORDER
   1. Social Responsibility
   2. The "Abundant Life"
   3. True Nationalism

VI. THE CHRISTIAN AND PATRIOTISM
   1. Patriotism Defined
   2. Patriotism and the Presidency
   3. Patriotism and the Supreme Court

QUESTIONS FOR REVIEW AND EXAMINATION

See Directions for the Teaching and the Study of This Book for Credit, page 113.

CHAPTER I

1. What is the background of religious nurture?
2. Discuss the Christian's initial experience.
3. What should be the attitude of members toward the church covenant?

CHAPTER II

4. Discuss the error of the "perfectionists" and the scriptural recipe for Christian character.
5. Tell of the practical means of Christian growth.
6. How is "sainthood" displayed?

CHAPTER III

7. What is the first requirement of stewardship?
8. Discuss the stewardship of the gospel.
9. How should Christians observe the Lord's Day?

CHAPTER IV

10. What is involved in the stewardship of possessions?
11. Name and discuss the principles of service.
12. How may Christians become channels of blessings?

CHAPTER V

13. Discuss responsibility for developing adult leadership.
14. Why should converts be promptly enlisted?
15. How may Christians engage in self-discipline?
16. Discuss corrective discipline.
17. Is punitive discipline needed in the churches of today?

CHAPTER VI

18. Discuss missions in the Bible.
19. Tell of missions in post-apostolic times.
20. Discuss modern missions and the organization of the Southern Baptist Convention.

21. Tell of the importance of state missions.
22. Describe religious conditions in the South and the work of the Home Mission Board.
23. Discuss Foreign Missions and the fields occupied by Southern Baptist missionaries.

CHAPTER VII

24. Are the teachings of Christ "too idealistic" for present-day Christians?
25. Discuss the sanctity of marriage.

CHAPTER VIII

26. What is the difference between liberty and tolerance?
27. Discuss the separation of church and state.
28. Discuss the Christian and the social order.
29. Discuss the Christian and patriotism.
30. How should Christians illustrate patriotism?

DIRECTIONS FOR THE TEACHING AND THE STUDY OF THIS BOOK FOR CREDIT

I. *Directions for the Teacher*

1. Ten class periods of forty-five minutes each, or the equivalent, are required for the completion of the book for credit.

2. The teacher of the class is given an award on the book if he requests it.

3. The teacher shall give a written examination covering the subject matter in the textbook, and the student shall make a minimum grade of 70 per cent. The examination may take the form of assigned work to be done between the class sessions, or as a final examination at the end of the course.

Exception: All who attend all of the class sessions; who read the book through by the close of the course; and who, in the judgment of the teacher, do the classwork satisfactorily may be exempted from taking the examination.

4. In the Graded Training Union Study Course, a seal for Course III, The Christian Life, is granted to Adults for the completion of this book.

Sunday school credit may be elected by the pupil. Application for Sunday school awards should be sent to the state Sunday school department and for Training Union awards to the state Training Union department. These departments will provide the forms for these applications. They should be made in duplicate and both copies sent.

II. *Directions for the Student*

1. In Classwork

(1) The pupil must attend at least six of the ten forty-five minute class periods to be entitled to take the class examination.

(2) The pupil must certify that the textbook has been read. (In rare cases where pupils may find it impracticable to read the book before the completion of the classwork, the teacher may accept a promise to read the book carefully within the next two weeks.)

(3) The pupil must take a written examination, making a minimum grade of 70 per cent. (All who attend all of the class sessions; who read the book through by the close of the course; and who, in the judgment of the teacher, do satisfactory classwork may be exempted from taking the examination.)

2. In Individual Study by Correspondence

Those who for any reason wish to study the book without the guidance of a teacher will use one of the following methods:

(1) Write answers to the questions printed in the book, or

(2) Write a development of the chapter outlines.

If the first method is used, the student will study the book and then with the open book write a development of the chapter outlines.

In either case the student must read the book through.

Students may find profit in studying the text together, but where awards are requested, individual papers are required. Carbon copies or duplicates in any form cannot be accepted.

All written work done by such students on books for Sunday school credit should be sent to the state Sunday school secretary. All of such work done on books for Training Union credit should be sent to the state Training Union secretary.

III. *Interchange of Credits and Awards on Comparable Subjects*

One award, either for Training Union or Sunday school, is granted for completing this book.

J. E. LAMBDIN
Secretary
Training Union Department
Baptist Sunday School Board

C. AUBREY HEARN
Director of the Study Course